LEADING PERFORMANCE...
BECAUSE IT CAN'T BE MANAGED

How to Lead the Modern Workforce

LARRY G. LINNE & DREW YANCEY

authorHOUSE

AuthorHouse™
1663 Liberty Drive
Bloomington, IN 47403
www.authorhouse.com
Phone: 833-262-8899

Published by AuthorHouse 08/18/2022

ISBN: 978-1-6655-6632-2 (sc)
ISBN: 978-1-6655-6633-9 (hc)
ISBN: 978-1-6655-6631-5 (e)

Library of Congress Control Number: 2022913984

Print information available on the last page.

CONTENTS

**Part III Field Guide to the Reverse
Performance Leadership System**

ACKNOWLEDGMENTS

Saying thank you at the beginning of a book is a challenge because I have gratitude for every person who has touched my life. A few people have made contributions more specific to *Leading Performance ... because It Can't Be Managed*, and I want to thank them.

Drew Yancey has become an incredible business partner to me over the past three years. When I first met him, I realized I wanted to be his business partner after I'd filled multiple pages of a journal with notes from our conversation. Drew, you are smart and will accomplish things I never dreamed possible. Thank you for your input and work on this book. When we work together, iron is sharpening iron!

Debi, you allow me to grow and challenge me to grow. I write because you teach me. Anna, thank you for your partnership and for keeping Drew grounded!

Maura, Bonita, Gordon, Ernestine, Renee, Max, Stephen, we think different because we choose to think critically and challenge ourselves. I am better because of each of you.

Leading Performance ... because It Can't Be Managed is complete because of Jim and Mike Kapnick, Mike Ross, Vaughn Troyer, Brian Long, Stephen DeMatteo, the York International management team, Robert Kestenbaum, Alex Meier, Bill Cameron, Dudley Wooley, Chip Gibson, Bill Rue, Greg Lottes, Tom Hickey, Brandon Mueller, Carl Bloomfield, Mike Taylor, Don Mills, Dean Hildebrandt, and Jessica Jung. Each of these people contributed with amazing feedback, stories to support our efforts, and opportunities to do unique things in our consulting practice.

All of our clients at InCite Performance Group, you are great at what you do because you realize the power of people and risk management. Performance leadership continues to be my passion because of your performance!

INTRODUCTION

A MAJOR SHIFT IN EMPLOYEES IS CHANGING EVERYTHING

The business world has seen a dramatic employee shift in the labor markets in the past twenty years. Beginning in the early 2000s, a company-centered market began to fade. Employee loyalty is no longer a given. We are now in an employee-centered market, putting the focus on personal brand, goals, growth and development, résumé building, and lifestyle.

The change didn't happen overnight. The dot.com era created new opportunity. Jobs became more plentiful and young people entered the market with a different view of work. These young workers didn't relate to work like their parents and prior generations did. Their parents identified themselves with the work and how they made a living. The new generation saw themselves as more than the job and identified the job as something they did to create an opportunity to define themselves in other areas of life. Workers were now realizing how easy it was to switch jobs for better opportunity, personal development, and making a better life.

Many people lost their jobs in the Great Recession of 2008 because companies could no longer afford them or had no need of them. Employees realized it was not a one-sided loyalty equation and that they had the same right-to-work contract as the employer.

However, many employers misread these changes as a lack of loyalty from employees, as entitlement, and as even new immature behavior. Because of this misread, the majority of employers missed a huge opportunity to keep people. The reality was that employees left jobs more often because they weren't being led by their supervisors in a manner that would benefit them. This is why we read numerous works on employees leaving supervisors and not jobs.

My observation in the current environment is that employees leave because supervisors have overwhelming command-and-control attributes. They don't find ways to develop employees or take the opportunity to meet the employee's needs. They also don't provide clear expectations or address intrinsic motivation, which creates a lack of engagement. In other words, they are trying to manage performance rather than lead it. Rather than think critically about how these changes could be leveraged to build stronger employees, business leaders have simply accepted them.

I would argue that we could have kept a large portion of these people had we changed how we led and managed. Leadership and management didn't shift with employee needs, and the consequences have cost trillions of dollars in turnover and lost productivity.

In March 2020, we experienced the pandemic and a dramatic increase in remote work. This shocking moment accelerated the changing beliefs and behaviors of employees. It also created new preferences: more autonomy, flexible work environments, and less travel.

I have advised many companies on how to navigate these challenges. Most businesses are taking an approach of mandating policy and work environment rules. But this approach completely misses the magnetic work environment people are looking for and instead forces a mandated environment where people are told what to do and how to do it.

It is interesting to hear executives speak of the need to have people "in the office," while key employees are being poached by competitors offering work-from-home opportunities. Traditional executives are adamant that their industry requires people to be in the office, but competitors are figuring out methods of getting the job done with remote systems.

It is not that the new models are working extremely well with no negative consequences. Reports are coming out frequently about worker burnout, depression and anxiety, social challenges, lack of collaboration, and many other consequences. Thus, we are facing even more challenges we must address.

However, stories are also being told of new technology solutions for increased collaboration, better work-life balance, and mental health support. Companies that leverage critical thinking skills and challenge their own biases are experiencing strong employee attraction and retention, increased productivity, and high grades for employee engagement.

I was recently on a video chat with a great friend and client, Jim Kapnick, and we were addressing many of the modern employee changes and challenges. Jim runs a large insurance agency in southern Michigan and is a great leader. He had attended an industry event where a speaker gave a very compelling argument about how the new employee environment demands flexibility of choice and independent decision-making.

I quickly responded, "Jim, that is exactly why we need to provide clarity of expectations to our people. If they are going to have more freedom on work hours, location, and even methods to get results, we must be clear on the results we expect and are willing to pay to receive."

Jim agreed and asked if I could help him get that done in his firm.

As I thought about the quick conclusion I had given Jim on performance leadership, I realized that most of the behavioral and mental shifts in employees over the past twenty years could be addressed with a leadership approach focused on helping employees maximize performance in their jobs.

What if we became leaders who gave clear expectations? What if we shifted management roles to focus on guaranteeing that employees were trained and developed? What if we could give more control to them in terms of flexibility, freedom, and decision-making? What if we shifted from performance management (mandates and control) to performance leadership and dramatically increased performance? Could we change the way people think about work and build new employee loyalty and increase performance at the same time?

I am convinced the answer is yes!

However, the biggest question is, what if we don't do anything different? What if we keep reacting and allow people to scramble with very little clarity and hope they are successful? How will that work out for us and our people?

I have a twenty-five-year history of thought leadership development in the performance leadership space. This conversation with Jim made me realize it was time to share my knowledge with the world through a book. I have also included the incredible work my business partner Dr. Drew Yancey has been doing implementing vivid vision and objectives and key results (OKRs) through strategic planning and execution.

It is our objective in *Leading Performance ... because It Can't Be Managed* to reveal twenty-five years of work on a system that has dramatically improved performance of individuals, teams, boards, companies, and even marriages.

We will offer concepts that will dramatically reduce time spent on performance management and reviews. We will introduce intellectual property on reverse performance management, discuss unique ways to measure performance, and address some of the most critical employee issues with huge behavior shifts in the past twenty years. The teaching in *Leading Performance ... because It Can't Be Managed* will allow for the transformation of the performance of a company and address the complex challenges of the shift in how our workforce thinks and acts.

Leading Performance ... because It Can't Be Managed is structured into three parts:

Part I. The Performance Leadership Problem

This segment addresses the reasons why performance cannot be managed. We will address the problems that have brought us to our current employee–employer relationship.

Part II. Reverse Performance Management

This segment provides clarity on how to solve the problems. Unique thought leadership is offered, and we give clarity of how to impact performance of individuals at a high level.

Part III. Field Guide to the Reverse Performance Leadership System

This segment will serve as a working guide for years to come. Included here is step-by-step how-to information on unique methods measuring almost anything, guides on frequency of meetings, sample performance objectives, success stories, and useful resources to build a successful performance leadership system.

You can also go to Intellectual-Innovations.com and receive additional resources to support your reading.

PART I

THE PERFORMANCE LEADERSHIP PROBLEM

CHAPTER 1

CLARITY OF THE PROBLEM WE MUST SOLVE, OR SHIFTS IN EMPLOYEE BELIEFS AND BEHAVIORS

Employees want flexibility, personal growth, that their intrinsic needs be met, the ability to do work how they best see fit, training and education, a job with purpose, and life balance.

That's a big list. Many employers will ask why they should be required to do all these things for an employee. The answer is simple: if you want the best talent that will get you the best results, you will have to be attractive to that group of people.

Building a magnetic culture that includes flexibility, choice, and a perception of control must be a company's strategic priority.

The concept for reaching this goal is similar to what psychologists have taught about managing children. If you tell them what to do, they will throw a fit, be angry, and fight against your suggestion. However, if you give them choices and options, they will pick between those options and be happy. The happiness comes from having control to make decisions, as opposed to being told what to do.

Our employees want options, choices, and flexibility on when and how they do things. We will be required to give clear expectations of the desired results and will need to provide training and support to help them accomplish those results.

Engagement and Training

My team has facilitated dozens of employee engagement surveys in the past two years. The results of every one of these surveys showed that employees desire and need more personal and professional development.

However, the employees also said they do not have the time to do this development.

My observation is that employees in command-and-control environments do not have the time to learn and improve because the entire focus of a manager is on workflow, meetings, and production. In a model where managers are focused on development of talent to perform, they would focus on training, coaching, and development of their people and would have greater results. This structure gives employees the belief that learning is acceptable and a function of the job.

However, the developmental model requires that employees have very clear expectations as to the desired results. Employees are focused on results, and managers are focused on coaching, training, motivation, and the tools to get the job done. The employees believe the manager is there to help them be successful instead of monitoring their output.

It seems the difference between these two models of management is that the culture (beliefs and behaviors that are normal) of command and control is focused on work product, whereas the culture with a training, coaching, and development management model prioritizes self-improvement and performance. However, this leaves the need for clarity of results to be put in place—and employees must own the outcomes and results in their job responsibilities.

Picture an NFL team. The desired outcomes are clear to the players. The position coaches are like managers in a work environment. Their job is to coach players to success. They do systems, design plays, and develop their processes after hours. In most work environments, managers don't have time for people during work hours. All the effort of an NFL coach during work time with players is to help those players become the best they can be.

This shift in the relationship of manager and worker will take purposeful change and a lot of hard work on the culture of a firm. We may have to make tough people decisions in management jobs. Managers will need to have a different skill set to be successful as coaches and trainers of people.

Manager Time and Skill

In my many years of business consulting, I have seen managers at hundreds of companies labor through annual reviews. They spend countless hours sifting through performance systems to determine the feedback they want to give to employees. They seek out ways to be objective. They look through reports. They ask for feedback from others about each employee. They stress about the compensation discussion and about the overall conversation. They hate this part of the job and it can be the most stressful task they perform.

I will argue the stress exists for three reasons:

The first stress driver is time. Managers know they will spend weeks of time and energy, only to return to a backlog of their own day-to-day responsibilities.

The second driver is lack of clarity of objective performance standards for the employee. So the managers are now in a position of having to give feedback that is subjective. This requires a lot of supporting research and thinking through all the potential arguments.

The third driver is a lack of training and knowledge on how to deliver proper feedback to employees on performance. We put people in these management jobs, but how many of them have been through any training on how to give proper feedback? How many know how to negotiate these discussions properly? I believe we set most managers up for failure with the typical performance management models.

Why would any manager look forward to employee feedback sessions under these conditions, knowing he or she is potentially going to have difficult conversations that he or she is not equipped to handle properly?

The structure is unproductive and, I believe, one of the causes of employee turnover. It is not fair to the employee or the manager.

Generational Evolution

This is not the first time in history we have seen a generational change in thinking. However, the nature and intensity of the shifts is unprecedented.

Technology is clearly the cause of most of the changes in today's work environment. Workflows change with new generations, even though many baby boomers try to keep the old workflows and just add the use of technology.

I hear my teenage and adult daughters question almost daily how people do things. They possess an instinct to ask, *How can I do that easier or faster?* This is not how older generations were trained. We were taught to follow the procedures and manuals and not question the smart people who created those models. Lean systems were introduced thirty-plus years ago, but very few work environments adopted those principles beyond a project or two.

Technology is also changing the mental makeup of employees. The constant notifications and dopamine hits that come from the stimulation from our phones or computers are changing how we think.

AI is narrowing and strengthening the biases of people and making change harder than it has been. We are losing critical thinking skills, and that is making people and companies ignorant. Companies who develop critical thinking will have a competitive advantage over those who allow this deterioration to occur.

These AI-driven dopamine hits are causing attention and focus issues as well. We have a harder time keeping people focused and productive.

Diversity

Gender, race, and generational and geographical diversity are influencing how people work. New ideas and influences are challenging traditional business models and work cultures. Employees want more input into how and where they do work. Employers who are listening and accepting the influence of diversity are accomplishing better results.

I just took a course on corporate governance at Wharton Business School. The instructors showed evidence of how increased diversity created more disagreement and, in some cases, increased time to make good decisions. However, the decisions were more effective and brought better results.

I was challenged early in my life to surround myself with people who didn't think the same as I did. I have applied that principle consistently, and I consider it to be the primary reason for my current level of intelligence and overall success. I spend time every day with people who make me uncomfortable and challenge my ideas. It is hard! But it has given me the opportunity to break ignorant biases and see new realities that create outstanding innovation and results.

Thirty years of marriage to a Hispanic woman, having five daughters who share that heritage, having strong women as business partners in our companies, and because of my fortunate sports experience of having close relationships with black men and their families have all shifted my thinking dramatically! My companies make decisions that dominate the competition, and we do things many companies simply cannot do, which I credit to the diversity in my life and my businesses.

My life experiences and relationships have made me aware of the lack of diversity in the work environment and thus the inability to address how diverse employee needs are being met.

The element of diversity is not "woke philosophy." I am speaking of the truths that exist where people who think differently can bring new perspectives and eliminate ignorant bias that permeates nondiverse environments.

The reality is that good companies with diverse employees are looking at work differently and are also looking for more flexibility in how we get work product completed.

The Need for Leadership

Strong leadership is essential in a rapidly changing world. The majority of people do not know how to navigate the challenges that exist in the workplace. Great leadership understands the challenges, and though great leaders may not have all the answers, they will help navigate to great outcomes.

Unfortunately, in most environments we have associated leadership with activities and not with results. People in leadership positions refer to their education, life events, books read, and social media posts to define their leadership. I was taught at an early age that a leader is one who is followed. Therefore, a great business leader is someone who is followed toward the desired results of the organization.

Our people need leaders to shift to results-based models.

Conclusion

The changes in the work environment, in people, in leadership, and in overall society have created a different workforce. The people of this workforce need flexibility, the ability to make decisions on how they get work done, freedom to have life balance, and probably new items we haven't learned yet.

On the other hand, companies need performance to compete in this complex and highly competitive world. This is not optional if we are going to survive economically. With command-and-control management fading fast, we need something that will allow leaders to lead where people will have a desire to follow.

The answer to this conundrum is clarity of expectations. People will need to know the outcomes required for success and will need to have the freedom to perform with flexibility, and supervisors will need to focus on development, coaching, and support.

We must create magnetic organizations vs mandate driven companies who tell employees what to do. A magnetic organization will attract people because they want to be there, and they want to perform at the highest level possible.

With very low unemployment, we need to recruit and retain the best people. We will need to create environments focused on development, personal growth, promotion, and clarity of expectations. Without these items in place, we will find high turnover, high costs, and overworking good people because of a lack of people and will potentially put our businesses at risk.

I hope you enjoy the stories and arguments gained by my and Drew's experiences, along with extensive research and work that will show you a better way to gain great performance in your organization.

CHAPTER 2

MY FIRST PERFORMANCE REVIEW

Performance management has been a passion of mine since 1988. It all began on the receiving end of my first real job employee performance review.

When I was hired, my supervisor told me I would have a performance and pay review at six months. Just past six months, I asked him when that was really going to happen. I was already frustrated because I wanted a raise and felt I was due one. He put me off for just over a month, then we finally met. I had a poor attitude going into the meeting because I already felt that he didn't care about me.

It may not have been fair for me to be upset with my supervisor, because my prior career had given frequent and clear feedback. I had been pursuing an NFL career the prior two years with three teams. The professional sports world gives immediate feedback on all performance. The fans provide boos, cheers, and a lot of advice. The coaches are typically screaming and always offer immediate feedback. A player never had to wait for a meeting to hear how he or she was doing.

No matter what caused my negative mindset, I was very upset with my supervisor because he had promised to give me feedback and a potential pay increase, and his being late on that commitment was all it took to make me feel unimportant.

The review began, and it consisted of three things I had done well and three things I needed to improve. Everything on the list was from the prior sixty days and was superficial and subjective. I could tell my supervisor hadn't thought about my performance anywhere near how I had thought about it. His comments were not well thought out and clearly were a sign of his checking a box and trying to justify the meager compensation he was offering.

I had performed at a higher level in that six-to-eight-month period than any other person in the department (measured sales results) and put in much more effort. Having seen a couple of my long-tenured coworkers' paychecks on their desks, I knew they made substantially more than I did.

So, when my supervisor gave me a 2 percent salary increase, I was less than impressed. I told him he should probably keep the raise because the company obviously needed that money more than I did. I left the building and spent the next two weeks looking for a job.

I don't blame that supervisor now, as I guarantee he had never been trained in performance management. With no solid system in place and given the corporate rules, he had done what he knew to do. However, the outcome gave me a terrible distaste for employee reviews, and I swore I would change that with my future work in leadership.

In the ensuing years, I saw models of performance management that were nothing more than a waste of time. These systems didn't improve performance, didn't give clarity on what really mattered, and didn't provide meaningful discussion on compensation. These terrible systems caused people to look for other jobs, made them feel unappreciated, lacked depth, and caused companies to spend hundreds of hours of management time administrating and executing ineffective processes.

Systems are used that cause managers to give feedback, and these managers do not have the training and skills to do it effectively. These reviews are a contest between the supervisor to give feedback that will support the compensation discussion or simply finally give some corrective feedback and the employee's justifying his or her quality of work and a potential raise. Before any feedback is given in the review, both sides are stressed and prepared to give their side of an argument from their respective positions. How in the world does this improve performance? The chance either will meet the other's expectations are next to zero unless the manager takes the path of least resistance and caves in to say only good things and give an unjustified raise.

Add to this problem that most employees don't have any clarity as to what is expected and how their performance is measured by their supervisor.

In the past twenty-five years I have interviewed thousands of employees and hundreds of supervisors. I ask the employee to tell me what is expected in the job and how performance is measured, what gets them a raise and/or promoted, and what would get them fired. Then I ask the supervisor the same questions about the employee. In twenty-five years, I have never had the two reports match perfectly. This datum alone should tell us the reason for terrible performance management: people are guessing.

Have you ever heard the old manager motivation statement "If you are asked to jump, you should simply ask how high"? Well, the reality of most organizations is that they live out a concept that sounds more like, "You the employee should jump as high as you can and hope the supervisor doesn't ask for more!" I believe this is what employees believe as they work, but over time they start to think they should just do their best and be prepared to defend themselves in a review. Isn't that sad?

Hundreds of books have been written about the topic, and most take positions based on biases that I believe are inaccurate. One of the most common errors in thinking and teaching is "You can't measure everything" or "Some things can't be measured." I disagree, at least in the execution of measuring anything that matters. If someone can be terminated or held back in an organization (or promoted) based on some factor, then that factor can be measured. You can measure numbers, frequency of behaviors, execution against a plan, and feedback assessment changes, and also measure against an initial feedback base and measure changes. I have been challenged for twenty-five years on this topic and have yet to fail at finding an effective measurement. When we do finally find something that can't be measured, my guess is we will conclude it is something that is irrelevant to job performance.

We must fix performance problems and give people a system that will truly influence the behaviors that will guarantee their success.

CHAPTER 3

TRADITIONAL PERFORMANCE MANAGEMENT HAS FAILED

Performance management has been attempted in many forms. The objectives of these systems have been to grade outcomes to determine continued employment, score for compensation justification, allow for an annual feedback session, and occasionally influence performance.

EOS® (Entrepreneurial Operating System®) has a model of determining culturally designed objectives. They suggest asking three questions: Does the employee have the capability? Does he or she get it? Does he or she want it? These are very solid questions and a solid process to help understand some of the attributes of an employee's actual contribution and potential contribution to the company.

Many firms use goal setting as the performance measurement method. An employee can establish the goals he or she has in the job, and the company works with the employee to determine how he or she is performing toward reaching those goals. Accomplishing personal goals can help the employee feel good about their outcomes, but it may not make a meaningful impact on the organization's outcomes.

Occasionally a firm will give regular feedback throughout the year to keep employees engaged with the supervisor. This is certainly valuable and helps with engagement. However, the feedback tends to be random and short term focused and not clearly focused on desired results that were understood from the beginning of the measured time period.

As far as measurement systems, some performance management systems find a way to easily measure the numbers that can be accomplished. These items could include sales goals, profit objectives, and growth expectation—things that are easily quantifiable. But very few performance measurement platforms introduce creativity to determine ways to measure other important items of value.

Almost every performance management system I have seen seems unable to find a way to measure with objectivity. The systems move toward subjective measurements, or they don't measure at all. Supervisors will tell you that they can't measure certain things, but they certainly come to conclusions on firing, promoting, and disciplining based on something.

Most people dread performance reviews. They find them frustrating because they tend to be subjective and random, and the employee doesn't agree with the measurements or conclusion.

Employers dread reviews because they take hours to prepare, time to deliver, and time to document and follow up with action items and administration.

These two unwilling parties (supervisor and employee) come together in a scenario that almost certainly fosters disagreement, whether stated or not. The outcome will typically create lack of productivity from the employee and the employer.

When performance management is supposed to improve performance through clarity, feedback, focus, and development, why is it delivering the opposite?

There are complex reasons for why performance management is broken. The answer requires more sophistication and a thought process to develop objective expectations, achieve clear communication, train supervisors how to have leadership conversations, create systems that allow for monthly updates, and provide clear measurement models. And you will see in the next chapter that it even matters who does the measurements. We have a lot of work to do!

CHAPTER 4

ABUNDANCE VS. SCARCITY

When I think about scarcity and abundance, I think of Thanksgiving dinner. Every year my wife makes pumpkin pies. A few years we have had a couple of pies and a lot of people. It is a battle for my five daughters, my wife, other invitees, and me to figure out how big or small the piece of pie we each will receive. In other years my wife has made more pies than we could eat in a week. We all get more pie and have no concerns about what percent of a pie we get.

Scarcity is where someone is thinking about protecting from loss and/or getting what he or she deserves. Thus, a small piece of pie is what I fear the most!

Abundance is a mindset of creating more, accomplishing bigger things, and knowing in the end these things will have a much greater result. It is a happy day when I can have a small portion of the total available pies, I am stuffed, and we still have leftovers for breakfast!

I believe scarcity thinking is one of the most damaging influences on a business.

The mindset of a typical performance management system is based on scarcity. The focus is on correction and/or making sure every task is being communicated to the supervisor. The fear is that every activity possibly done is being clearly communicated upwardly and that every area of potential criticism is delivered to the employee from the supervisor. Every aspect of this exchange is draining and focused on protectionism.

When leaders and employees have an abundance mindset, they can look at the big picture of how behaviors and actions in a company can ultimately create much larger gains and overlook the little issues that seem on the surface to be deterrents to success. An abundance mindset allows employees to feel liberated from being required to give every detail of activity during a time period to try to justify their existence.

Don't get me wrong. I am not suggesting we ignore correction or mistakes. I am suggesting we take a bigger look at the impact of correction and the discipline of decision-making that creates a balance toward a greater good.

Consider a supervisor going into an annual performance review. The employee performed at a reasonable level as it was subjectively measured. The supervisor has only 3 percent available for a potential pay increase. The employee wasn't perfect and made a few mistakes, so there are areas available to criticize during the performance period. The scarcity mindset would have the supervisor emphasize the negative issues out of balance with the positives so he or she can justify the 3 percent pay increase. Positive items would be left out or deemphasized to leverage against the employee's arguing for more pay.

An abundance thinking strategy would start with a focus on getting the best performance out of the employee. It would emphasize elements that create energy for the employee. It would realize if the right performance objectives were in place, the results would allow for payment of raises that represent the performance. The positive nature of a system that developed the employee, encouraged him or her, and gave him or her clear targets that were objective would potentially guarantee higher levels of performance.

Another example of scarcity performance management is gleaned from a story I recently heard from a business executive in the automotive repair industry. He told me that his technicians at one of his shops had the most productive month in the shop's history. They hit a record revenue and profit number. However, the controller came to him and said the technicians had spent one hundred dollars on a food delivery services. This was not company policy, and the controller felt they should charge it back to the technicians.

The executive had a much different, abundant thought about that experience. He said, "I think the sixty-six thousand dollars of revenue with exceptional profit is due to the incredible productivity of these guys. If they'd had to clock out and go eat lunch or send a technician to get food for everyone, we would have made less money."

I have worked with many supervisors who are afraid of complimenting, recognizing, or praising an employee for doing something well because the employee has other areas in which he or she needs to improve. These supervisors seem to think the employee will relax and stop working on improvement if they feed him or her a compliment. This is scarcity thinking.

Many people in management positions tend to be quick to criticize or notice a need for correction and *very* slow to praise and show appreciation.

The concept of focusing on the negatives vs. the positives is true for individuals as they evaluate themselves as well. Most humans emphasize correction of behavior and fixing problems much more than they celebrate success. I find that in my own life.

Recently I gave a presentation at an event. The session required very specific timing, and I had to be finished at an exact time. It was a TED talk–style speech, with three speakers scheduled to speak in a single hour. It was critical that each speaker finish on time so the next person would start on time. We had all committed to make this happen.

I was the first of the three. The session started. The host spoke for a few minutes and then introduced another surprise: they had a sponsor and needed to do a quick commercial. I was finally introduced and had fifteen and a half minutes to deliver a twenty-minute speech. Unfortunately, at nineteen minutes I realized I was not yet on my final point. I went past the timing by two minutes and spewed out a very uncompelling ending to my speech. I was devastated. Because I am a very disciplined speaker, I never run over my speech times. I spent the rest of the day and the entire weekend beating myself up about this terrible outcome.

The next morning, I went to the golf course and played a round with some friends. When we got to the ninth hole, I proceed to hit a beautiful 177-yard shot using an 8 iron—one hop, and in the hole. Yes, a hole in one! What a great experience! The odds are incredibly low for this to happen in someone's life. Excited, I celebrated the day and chose to buy quite a few drinks at the country club.

The rest of the story is that I continued to beat myself up all weekend about that speech. I believe I thought about my flub for hours the rest of the weekend. I spent a couple of hours addressing and remembering the hole in one. When I went to the office on Monday, all I could think about was my embarrassment at having going over the time limit for my speech. In summary, I spent hours beating myself up over a speech ending and gave myself only a fraction of the credit I deserved for an almost once-in-a-lifetime achievement (though it was my second ace).

This is how most people treat themselves. They overthink and dwell on the negative and give the positive too little notice and recognition.

This same mindset is behind how managers fail employees, but it is worse. The celebrations of success are much fewer because successes tend to be more expected and not appreciated with the same energy as failure is criticized. So, supervisors will tend to gloss over a win or success but won't let negative or poor performance experience leave their heads.

This desire to make sure everything is fixed will cause a supervisor to keep a cloud of negativity over the head of an employee for months, if not years. This is a very unbalanced relationship and results in a huge missed opportunity.

Many books have been written about the concept of being too critical vs. showing appreciation and giving praise. These books highlight how leaders should be slow to criticize and quick to praise. They speak about the importance of focusing on strengths as opposed to fixating on weaknesses.

After a career of more than thirty years of leadership and management, my experience proves that these positive theories of positivity and abundance leadership are better than negative and scarcity management.

Abundance gives energy. Scarcity drains people.

I worked at an insurance agency in a sales management role. One day I sent out an email to every person under my department (twenty-seven people). The email read, "Congratulations. Great job!" Emails started coming back immediately saying "Thank you," along with other responses indicating that I was accurate for recognizing the employee's achievement.

A few hours later we had a department meeting and I asked who had received this email. All the employees raised their hands. I asked them, "How many of you connected that recognition to a specific result you achieved?" Everyone raised their hand again. I explained the reason I sent the email. I sent it because I believe people do things daily that deserve positive recognition and appreciation. However, we don't give it to them.

I apologized for the insincerity of the original email and explained that it was research to prove to me and other managers how important it is for us to catch our people in the act of positive performance. I went to each person over the next few days to find out what they had done that deserved my praise, and we enjoyed amazing conversations.

I know from my own experience that when a supervisor hits me with criticism, I certainly accept it and work to improve the problem, but my energy drops hard. I want to go home and ride my bike or do something to get my mind off work. In contrast, when I get a compliment from my supervisor, my energy raises to a high level, and I find more to do that will bring more positive results.

I hear my adult children tell me about supervisors praising them or recognizing top performance. They are so pumped up and energized that they can't wait to get back to work the next day.

We have an opportunity to feed energy to our people if we will build energy-building automatic recognition into our performance management systems.

Removing scarcity thinking and creating an abundance mindset will generate exceptional results. Building abundance thinking and process into performance management systems will create an automated system of abundance results.

PART II

REVERSE PERFORMANCE MANAGEMENT

CHAPTER 5

THE BEGINNING OF REVERSE PERFORMANCE LEADERSHIP

Many rounds of golf have allowed me to spend time with very smart executives and successful businesspeople. I have learned quite a bit on the links after asking questions and listening to stories of success, innovation, and risk-taking. Some learned experiences are valuable lessons; most learning simply challenged my thinking and challenged me to grow. However, one day I played with Jim (I wish I could remember his last name to give him the credit he deserves), and he flipped my world upside down.

On the first tee box, we introduced ourselves and made typical excuses for our games. It was just the two of us, and the course was wide open. It was a beautiful New Mexico day at Four Hills Country Club. We both seemed ready for a relaxing round and possibly meeting a new friend.

As the district manager for Ryder Commercial Leasing and Services for New Mexico, West Texas, and southern Colorado at the time, I was responsible for 176 people in nine truck maintenance and rental facilities. Safety, risk management, and sales were always top of mind for me. When Jim said he was a safety culture consultant, it immediately triggered my interest and led me to ask business-related questions.

I asked, "What is a safety culture consultant, Jim?"

Jim responded by informing me that his title seemed to change as he evolved in his job. He said he recently had changed the title because he realized the world of safety was evolving to become a cultural issue and not just a training and management reporting function.

It was 1996. Safety culture work was certainly being written about and was becoming common in many organizations. It wasn't new, but he mentioned that he had found a unique strategy that moved the needle in the results of the US Air Force.

I realized at that point that he wasn't small time. If he was doing work with the US Air Force, then he was probably very credible.

I bit and offered up the appropriate question: "What happened with the Air Force?"

He said he had been hired to help with a facility on a base that was having poor safety results. The location was having high frequency and, unfortunately, too many high-severity injuries.

He went on to explain how they had applied modern safety training, incentive programs, new camera technology, drug testing, and just about every technique I had ever experienced or heard about with my safety background. However, the air force continued to have very little to no change in results, he said.

Jim had spent a few weeks in visual observation, met with all officers and staff, read reports, and asked every question he could about how the Air Force managed safety.

Very excited when he reached this point of the conversation, he said, "Larry, I was dreaming in the middle of the night, when the answer came to me clear as could be. They needed to flip the safety culture upside down."

I laughed and said, "That doesn't sound very safe!"

After a quick snicker, he agreed and told me about the magic he had uncovered.

The problem was who owned the measurement. He described how the top officers would get reports from HR on injury and claims. The data would come to them. They would meet with the officers below them, who would meet with the officers below them who supervised the mechanics, tire techs, other techs, fuel island personnel, et al.

So, the people who were getting injured and having incidents were getting told how they performed in safety, and it was usually weeks after the behavior had happened.

Jim said, "These guys didn't think about results while working. They just waited to be told if they were doing a good job or not a few weeks after they had acted in their jobs."

He concluded that the people who were at risk of injury needed to measure and monitor their own results and report up through the organization.

The next day he went to the facility and put a committee of frontline employees together: a few mechanics, parts personnel, techs, and other laborers. He created a form that had clear items to look for in a safe work environment, including cleanliness, using tire blocks when doing repairs, ensuring doors were shut on vehicles, ensuring equipment was in the proper place, wearing back braces when lifting, and wearing eye protection, among other things.

He taught them how to do a ten-minute walk around the facility and identify safe acts, unsafe acts, and components of the environment that would constitute either high or low risk of injury. Then, he told HR they needed to report all incidents and accidents to the committee. The committee would review the reports and focus on communication and training other team members in the facility immediately after learning of an incident. Then the committee would collect the information and track the results in a document. They would communicate results weekly to their supervisor. That supervisor would report the information up through the chain of command.

The Safety Tracking Committee, as it came to be named, would rotate a person off each month so all personnel would eventually serve on the committee.

The results: zero injuries. At the time of that day's round of golf, they had reached more than a year without an incident! Every time I saw Jim at the club, I would ask how it was going, and he would just give me the "okay" hand signal, meaning zero incidents/accidents.

He explained his conclusion: "When people own the results and expectations, measure the results, and have clarity of those expectations, they will act differently than they do when a supervisor knows the expectations and reports to people how they are doing."

We finished the eighteenth hole about the time he gave me the conclusion of his efforts and the results. My mind was racing because of a current Ryder national HR committee role. I had been placed on the national HR committee to rework the performance management systems for the company!

What amazing timing for this discussion!

I asked myself throughout Jim's describing of his experience, *What would be the difference between performance improvements in safety behaviors and performance in any job?* If someone owns the job, is measuring the results, and reports upward, wouldn't he or she be more in tune with the results and perform better? Wouldn't supervisors be more equipped to support the person as coaches, mentors, and trainers, versus being lord and master over the employee's performance?

I even questioned how many people in the workforce actually knew what results or outcomes were expected of them in their jobs. I knew salespeople in companies who were successful at selling but still lost their jobs. That must have meant more than just selling was expected. Maybe something was expected in terms of other behaviors or outcomes.

I went to the office Monday morning and went around to numerous employees and asked them, "What is expected of you in your job? How is it measured? And what would get you promoted or fired?"

I had written down on paper the answers to those questions for every person prior to asking them to answer. *Not one person's answers matched what I had written down!*

Oh my! How in the world could they meet expectations when they couldn't articulate clearly what was expected? In most cases they said things like, "I need to simply come in and jump as high as I can and hope my supervisor doesn't want more."

These employees were told how they were doing with some subjective, some objective, and some very random opinions from their supervisors. Bottom line, my team was surprised by the feedback. They feared reviews because they felt they needed to be prepared to defend themselves in all areas because they knew it would be subjective and random.

How in the world would they be successful in their performance if they weren't clear and weren't measuring their own performance?

I went to the national committee at Ryder and told them of this amazing revelation. They rejected it without even hearing my complete explanation. They were the experts, and it became clear I was just a token field person on the committee.

I was still convinced I had the answer. I went back to my company and started writing performance objectives. I started with me, then moved to my executive team, then managers, salespeople, and administrative staff, going straight through all employees. It took me two weeks to get all the objectives written. They were objective, with clear results, that answered a few questions:

1. What outcomes would make me happy that the person is in his or her job for the money he or she is being paid?
2. What results would the person need to accomplish in order to get promoted?
3. What results would the person have to accomplish to be removed from the job?

I delivered these objectives (I will explain in detail in a later chapter) to each team member and explained how the process would work:

1. They would be required to monitor and measure, with evidence, the results they were accomplishing within the agreed upon objectives.
2. They were required (as part of the objectives) to meet with their supervisor each month for fifteen minutes to show evidence of the results.
3. Supervisors would become coaches to help them accomplish their results. This meant they didn't have to do prep work on monthly feedback. They needed to listen and provide help (advice, counsel, training, ideas, etc.) to guarantee employee success.
4. Annually the supervisor would have an easy review after recording the results all year long (the employee would keep records as well).

Our results: we moved from being one of the lowest-performing districts in the United States to one of the top performers within the space of one year. After three months I began asking colleagues, "What is expected in your job, and how are you doing?" Every employee could tell me the answer without looking at reports. They knew the expectations and exactly how they were doing.

This became an energizing element of our firm. Everyone knew the desired results for their job; they managed to achieve those results; and supervisors supported them to reach the desired results. They *owned* the outcomes, and we experienced amazing results.

Jim left our golf club and I ended up moving away from Albuquerque, so I never had the opportunity to share with him how amazing his sharing of his experience changed my and my 176 employees' lives. Now I have introduced this concept to thousands of people, who are experiencing great performance because Jim taught me about reverse performance management.

Jim, thanks for your incredible wisdom! You flipped my world upside down!

CHAPTER 6

TAKE OUT THE TRASH

My father is a very big man, standing 6'7" tall and typically weighing about 240 pounds. He played in the NFL for the Baltimore Colts as a large tight end and oversized punter. The picture you have in your mind right now is what I pictured every time I was in trouble as a kid. I was never certain, but always thought it possible, he could crush me at a moment's notice if he ever decided it was necessary.

One fall morning my father loudly summoned me to come to the kitchen. Obviously, I quickly arrived and saw him standing next to our trash can.

The trash was overflowing. I immediately realized the purpose of my visit. It was my responsibility to take out the trash, and he was probably going to say something about it.

He was calm and kind that morning and decided to give me a lesson in accountability. He said, "This trash has been here for days. That is unacceptable. It is your job to take out the trash every day. If it doesn't go out, it will stink. I am leaving for my weekly trip, and when I get home on Sunday, you had better have taken this trash out every day. If you don't take it out, you will have big consequences."

My father owned a printing and publishing company. He published the football programs for the University of Texas, Baylor, SMU, Texas Tech, and the University of Oklahoma. Every Thursday he would leave Midland, Texas, with his big truck and drive to Fort Worth, where he would pick up programs and go deliver them to the universities. He liked doing that because he could choose a game and go on the sidelines and take pictures.

With my father's departure, I quickly went into action. I had a clear plan to impress my father with the greatest performance of my life! I went to work.

The first job I did was to clean all the leaves in our yard. The front was small but had a huge tree with all the leaves recently dropped. The backyard was very large with many trees. It was a full afternoon job to bag all those leaves.

While pulling leaves from the bushes at the back of the house, I noticed the window seals had paint cracking. I went to the garage and found some white paint. After sanding the window seals with cracks, I painted all of them with a shiny white coat of paint!

This was going amazingly. My father was going to be very proud of this great work I was doing.

On Saturday I decided to help my mom. My dad always appreciated when we kids did things to help her. So, I vacuumed the entire house. This was a big home with a lot of carpet. It took a good two and a half hours to complete the job.

The feeling of satisfaction was pretty grand when I was done with all the work. It made me feel as if I was contributing to the betterment of our family, and I finally was going to make my father proud with my home contribution. I could go to sleep that night with a sense of accomplishment.

My father would be home the next day. I was certain he would break out into the Hallelujah Chorus as soon as I told him of the hours of labor I had put in.

Sunday morning, I was upstairs in my bedroom when I heard the engine of his big truck driving up our street and into our driveway. I was excited to tell him about the amazing work I had done. He opened the front door and walked into the house, and about fifteen seconds later he barked loudly throughout the house, "Larry Glen Linne, get down here *now!*"

In that moment I realized I had *forgotten* to take out the trash!

My thoughts raced. *Oh no, is this my last day on earth.*

I walked slowly down the stairs gathering my thoughts. Then I realized that even if I hadn't took out the trash, he was going to be amazed at all I did.

When I arrived in the kitchen, my father looked quite upset. He asked me why I hadn't taken out the trash after he specifically had asked me to do so.

I went right into my explanation of all the great things I had done, expanding into the details of every activity. He stood and listened with patience. Then he taught me a foundational lesson.

He expressed the importance of every family member's having a job that made our home run efficiently. My taking out the trash was a function of health, safety, and good or bad smells next to our refrigerator and kitchen table. It was a core chore that had to be done daily.

He proceeded to explain what each family member did to keep the household running efficiently. Then he spoke of my hard work on the extra items.

He said, "Thank you for picking up the leaves, but I like to keep those leaves on the lawn during the winter. We live in West Texas, and it is dry. If the leaves stay on the ground, they tend to keep moisture in the ground better, reduce the freezing temperatures on the grass, and they break down into mulch for softening the soil."

Who knows if any of those items were effective, but he felt it was a good idea.

Then he said, "Thanks for the paint on the windows, but that wasn't really necessary." He also thanked me for vacuuming. But then he said, "If you wanted to do something extra, I would have asked you to clean the garage. That would have been the most helpful and would have made a real difference. I would have truly appreciated that work. Everything else was just nice, but it wasn't anything that made a big difference."

He reminded me again, "Until you take out the trash, nothing else matters!"

As I reflect on this experience, I am reminded of the countless employee reviews where an employee can't wait to meet with his or her supervisor to hear how great he or she has been as an employee. However, the supervisor is dreading the discussion with the employee because he or she didn't "take out the trash."

But was it the employee's fault? Did the employee understand and know what was expected? I certainly knew it was expected, but I didn't see the big picture of how it fit into the overall success of our family. It was just a chore to me.

We need to give people clarity in terms of the core results they must achieve and how those tasks fit into the big picture of the organization. When they have that clarity, then we need to give them guidance on the next best thing they can do to positively impact the organization (i.e., clean the garage).

CHAPTER 7

VIVID VISION AND OKRS START THE PROCESS

It is difficult for people to experience clarity within an organization if the organization itself doesn't have clarity. On average, only about 15 percent of employees report that they understand their organization's goals and how they contribute to those goals.

In order for an organization to establish clarity, four key questions need to be answered clearly and communicated consistently throughout the organization:

1. Values: Who Are We?

Values are shared beliefs and behaviors within an organization. They are not simply an embodiment of what we say we believe, but they represent how we actually behave. They are essential for clarity because they ultimately help an organization make decisions. What are we willing to lose customers and employees over? What are our nonnegotiables? These are our core values.

2. Purpose: Why Do We Exist?

Human beings crave purpose, especially in our work. Clear organizational purpose that speaks to what we value can motivate us to achieve amazing results and persevere through tough challenges. A lack of organizational purpose can cripple even the most talented individuals. The biggest mistake organizations make when identifying their purpose is to put themselves at the center. Rather, an organization needs a stakeholder-centered purpose. Every organization has at least two sets of stakeholders: external (i.e., customers) and internal (i.e., employees). An organization's purpose should compellingly capture the value it creates (or the problems it solves) for both external and internal stakeholders.

3. Objectives: Where Are We Going?

Values and purpose alone are insufficient to establish organizational clarity because they do not tell us where we are going or how are we going to get there. Objectives, or goals, articulate a clear future state. Objectives are not mere descriptions. They are aspirational and ambitious goals that ultimately answer the question, "What does amazing look like?"

This is one of the most powerful questions we could ever ask in business and in life. Recent organizational science has highlighted the benefits to organizations and people of having ambitious and aggressive goals. Human beings have a strong negativity bias. We naturally fear loss more than we strive for gain. By describing a vivid vision that connects values, purpose, and objectives, an organization can establish powerful clarity that compels individuals to unique levels of achievement and results. Much like with purpose, an organization should craft a vivid vision that speaks to its external and internal stakeholders. What are our key stakeholders saying about us when we achieve something amazing? How will the accomplishment of our important objectives create value for our stakeholders?

4. Strategy: How Are We Going to Get There?

Clear values, purpose, and objectives establish the foundation for organizational clarity. But in order for clarity to be lived out within an organization, the organization must also have a clear strategy. A strategy is a road map. It tells us how we are going to achieve the vivid vision.

One of the biggest mistakes organizations make with their strategy is thinking about strategy in terms of activities instead of results. The two are not the same. For example, if you are trying to summit a mountain and you're measuring progress based on how many steps your Apple Watch has tracked, is four thousand steps good? It depends on where those steps are taking you.

You could be working hard and getting nowhere. Unfortunately, that is where many organizations find themselves when it comes to their strategic plans. For too long, we have evaluated the quality of a strategic plan based on the number of priorities and activities needed to support those priorities. The more priorities, the better, right?

Organizational science suggests the opposite. Research by the consulting firm Strategy& found that there is an inverse relationship between the number of strategic priorities and an organization's revenue growth. Companies with fewer than six strategic priorities consistently outperformed, while those with more than six priorities reported higher levels of resource allocation challenges and organizational waste, and lack of clarity about whether their activities created value for stakeholders.

When we put the focus on results, it becomes clear that less is more. The world is increasingly complex and noisy. Organizational leaders have significant demands on their time and energy. A strategic plan should identify the vital few priorities and outcomes that warrant precious focus.

Identifying three to five vital few priorities is an important starting point for a strategic plan. But priorities and good intentions do not automatically translate into execution and results. To do this requires turning each priority into a clear goal.

An OKR (objectives and key results) framework ensures that a priority moves into an actionable goal with quantifiable outcomes. OKRs tell us that a priority becomes a goal when we have a clear objective with measurable key results. For example, for each priority, what does success look like (the goal), and how will you know if you have achieved success (the key results)?

An effective strategic plan does not sit on the shelf, only to be reviewed once or twice a year. It is a dynamic, living document meant to guide an association's ongoing prioritization and resource allocation. The OKR framework enables organizations to assess progress frequently so they can celebrate wins, identify potential roadblocks, and adjust in real time.

By establishing and communicating clarity in these four critical areas, organizations create an environment in which individual clarity and performance leadership can flourish. But how do we link organizational goals to individual goals? That is where performance objectives come in.

CHAPTER 8

PERFORMANCE OBJECTIVES ARE THE CONNECTOR

Most companies put together very detailed job descriptions. A job description explains the details of the work and the normal activities a person will do.

When I work with companies to help them with performance, I ask to see the job descriptions, performance objectives, strategic plans, and company goals. Most companies will show me the job descriptions, then pull out the company goals—and they *may* have some form of strategic plan. However, the documents rarely express clear performance objectives that describe what we expect from our people and how those objectives are measured.

When I interview employees about their job and ask what is expected of them, I seek to understand expectations and measurements for success. Unfortunately, the responses are usually blank stares. They just do the job. They aren't able to connect the dots to the corporate goals.

I asked a receptionist one time how the profit, revenue growth, and client experience goals of the company were being met by her in her job. She said, "That isn't my job. I just answer the phones."

I explained to her that if she were to answer the phone poorly, they could lose clients. If she answered phones timely, asked great questions, made sure the client arrived at the right place when transferred, and didn't keep people on hold, then the clients would have a great experience. That great experience would be an influence in retention, new sales, and overall client experience. However, I had to explain the outcomes and results of the job description for her to make the connection. I will give more details pertaining to this example in the chapter on writing performance objectives.

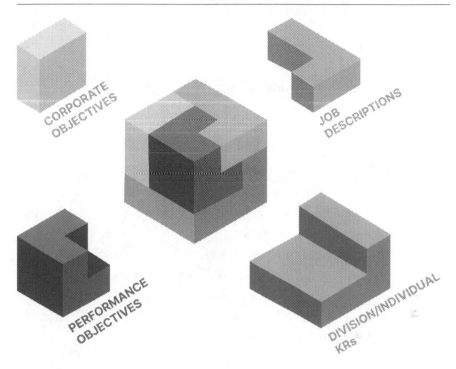

Performance objectives are the connection between job descriptions, company objectives, and key results. In my company we have four steps:

1. Identify corporate objectives.
2. Set division/individual KRs
3. Clarify performance objectives.
4. Write job descriptions.

Corporate objectives are identified measurable objectives that must be met to accomplish "What does amazing look like?"

Group/division KRs are the measurable key results that must happen within a subgroup or division for the organization to meet its strategic objectives.

Individual KRs (objectives and key results) are the connection of individual outcomes specifically to division or corporate OKRs.

Performance objectives describe the specific performance outcomes and results that will be measured to discern effective individual contribution to the company. If the person is a manager, he or she will typically have a large weighted objective related to the responsibility to meet the divisional or corporate OKRs.

A job description provides clarity on the common activities that are part of the job. It describes work activities and engagements and explains typical skills required to do the job effectively.

The reason for the extra step is because OKRs do not give the complete picture of what we expect from a high-performing employee. Being a good corporate citizen, achieving individual performance on teams, and serving functions that assist in accomplishing an OKR can be measured and will create more success when those items are identified. So, our teammates have objectives, with one or more objectives being the accomplishment of the OKRs. We also weight these items so the OKRs can be a heavy influence, but our overall goals are met more successfully when we have a clear picture of all OKRs and individual performance objectives.

CHAPTER 9

NAMING HISTORY

When I originally developed this model of performance management, I was asked by dozens of businesses familiar with our results to help them create a similar model for them.

One of my first clients was a flower shop in Albuquerque, New Mexico. The owner was a golf friend and very successful entrepreneur. I went through the process with him and his executive team. We developed all the objectives, and I suggested we do training with all the managers.

Every store manager and the executive staff, other than the CEO, was female.

I opened the session and introduced the concepts I have been sharing thus far in *Leading Performance ... because It Can't Be Managed.* Then I revealed the name of the product Impact Performance Management System™. Yes, the logo was on the cover of all the documents. I taught the program for the first hour and then gave the attendees a break. There was a lot of laughing and talking going on during the break. Finally, one of the leaders came to me and said, "You may want to consider changing the name of the program. I don't think many people will feel good about 'I-PMS.'" She said, "The jokes are overwhelming the content at this point. The fear of a new performance measurement system feels a little like PMS!"

That was the last day we called the program IPMS. We shifted to Reverse Performance Management™. It has stayed that way to this day in July 2022.

In February 2022 I was in Westchester, New York, with one of my best and favorite clients. York International is an amazing insurance agency. They have some of the most impressive executives I have worked with in my career.

As I was introducing the Reverse Performance Management system to them, we became very engaged in deep dialogue about the concept. At one point they inspired me to respond, "In today's work environment, we really can't manage the performance of others. What we must do is lead them to perform."

I paused and wrote "performance leadership" on the whiteboard. I looked at the group and said, "I am changing the name again. From now on I will call this system Reverse Performance Leadership."

This is a significant move because I do not believe it is reasonable or logical in today's work environment to expect to manage someone else's performance. We must lead performance. That means we must give people clear objectives, training and development, feedback, coaching, and resources and then be an example to them with our own performance.

We must hire people who are committed to performance and results.

Leaders will be required to lead to desired outcomes. This method is going to expose those who don't truly know how to lead. Managers who intimidate to get work done will fail. Managers who are lazy and are unwilling to take the time to give clarity to others will fail. Managers who aren't willing to invest time and resources into the development of people will fail.

The system we are introducing in *Leading Performance … because It Can't Be Managed* will give people who are committed to leadership the ability to lead people who are results oriented.

CHAPTER 10

LEADERSHIP PROBLEMS IN PERFORMANCE MANAGEMENT

Inexperienced and Untrained

I have met hundreds of managers who have never been trained on how to have tough conversations, deliver bad news, encourage employees, correct them, or develop them.

The odds are high that anyone in a management role is there because he or she was good at the job and had been promoted to manage people who do that job. This is not new information. We have all heard about managers having all the skills to do the subordinates' jobs but having zero skills in leadership and management.

We put these inexperienced people across from those who really care about the feedback they receive and who feel their future is in the hands of this unqualified person who will tell them how they are doing.

The manager must find things to talk about. He or she will most likely look at the past sixty days because that is as far as he or she can easily remember. The manager may remember something really big from farther back, but the immediacy of the review requires him or her to give clear feedback that is relatable.

If the feedback is positive, the manager will probably overstate how wonderful the person is doing. This is a feel-good method for giving feedback that gets one through the conversation easily and allows the box to be checked. But it misses the opportunity to share where the employee may be falling slightly short or where he or she could improve and do great things. This could potentially turn the employee into a lesser performer because he or she will think too highly of himself or herself from that inaccurate feedback. Then when the negative items become a frustration or magnify, the manager will address them, and it will be a big surprise.

If the feedback is negative, the employee must argue and fight back (or just get mad and leave and never say anything), because he or she is protecting his or her income and job. The lack of objectivity sets the person up to defend himself or herself based on whatever playing field he or she so chooses. Some managers feel compelled to point out the negatives of people and won't spend any quality time on the positive attributes and performance of the individual.

I have had managers tell me, "I don't want to compliment employees too much because I really need them to work on these issues that I want them to improve." Though the manager may have a balanced view of the person, the employee will not perceive that based on the heavily weighted time and energy spent on the negative.

I have done a lot of marriage counseling in my life. One common reason for relationship breakups is when the couple focuses on each other's weaknesses, not their strengths. They quickly point out what they don't like and lose sight of what they love. I encourage those couples to seek what they love and then be honest about what frustrates them. When they do this, these couples find that the criticisms become fewer in this model because the balance allows for the relationship to allow trust to drive the conversation.

I believe business relationships are very similar. A leader earns the right to give criticism when he or she shows he or she cares about the other person. Showing that he or she cares starts with giving clear expectations. The caring continues with proper and accurate feedback that is intended to help the employee have success. Finally, the corrections are welcomed as long as the balance against accuracy of expectations is communicated, and coaching and development is offered.

Lack of Clarity Is a Common Reason for Any Failure in Relationships

I have asked hundreds of supervisors over the past twenty years the following question: "If the objectives are not clear, when will you make the decision to speak to an employee about an area where you feel he or she is falling short?"

The answer is always the same: "When I get angry or frustrated enough to talk to the employee about it."

Doesn't that sound like a recipe for failure? Can you imagine that being the trigger for any controversial conversation? Anger, frustration, oh my!

Most of the time an untrained supervisor will typically avoid a difficult conversation if the negative feedback is not bad enough to make him or her mad or angry enough to address. He or she will either not talk about it or potentially make passive-aggressive statements about it to try to introduce the topic. Either way, it will turn out a bad result.

A performance review meeting has a great chance of negativity without clear expectations or clear measurements and with an untrained manager who is winging employee feedback. Some companies make it worse. They believe an untrained manager can't do these sessions alone, so they bring in HR to be part of the meeting. This intimidates the employee and makes him or her defensive from the start.

Every performance management system I have seen is either a nice goal-setting session that will make almost zero impact on the employee's performance or is structured to create a defensive conflict-filled discussion where the parties are there to argue a position that may or may not align. In the end, the outcome typically is not going to be good.

I have served on numerous business and charity boards of directors. On every board, I have seen frustration from board members pertaining to each other and between the board and the executive staff. One hundred percent of the time it is because of a lack of clarity on how expectations are measured. A board will typically have a few highly experienced executives as members. These people have expectations that come with those experiences. The executive director is required to guess and do his or her best with the hope that he or she will meet the subjective and uncommunicated objectives of the board members.

It shouldn't surprise anyone to know that when I challenge the group to come to clear measurable objectives for the executive team, the discussion is challenging because of all the different views.

Once again, how can anyone, a spouse, a child, an employee, a board member, a teammate, accomplish success when the expectations are unknown?

Entitlement

Another problem with managers is entitlement.

Most people would read that statement and say, "Yes, the young people nowadays are so entitled!"

However, that is not what I am speaking about with regard to entitlement. I am speaking about reverse entitlement.

I get in a lot of trouble with this concept, but I will defend it to the end of time.

I define entitlement as expecting something because you feel as if you are owed or deserve something without earning it.

The number of times I have seen managers who act entitled to receive great performance from employees far outweighs the number of times I have seen entitled employees.

Management entitlement, or reverse entitlement, is a concept I began teaching in 2005. I was listening to a group of CEOs talk about how entitled the young employees were in their organization. They were not wrong in what they were saying. The entitlement examples were real and very accurate.

As I listened to these CEOs, I realized they thought they deserved and were owed the loyalty and top performance of their people without doing anything to deserve it. They assumed that giving someone a job and pay was good enough to get that person's best.

Watch professional athletes and you will see that top performance isn't something guaranteed by pay and a job. A coach was most likely involved in increasing the performance. Look at employees in most firms and you will probably find that most of the time that the people who perform at high levels exist where a leader earns that performance.

Leading performance starts with clarity of expectations, which is then followed by development, feedback, encouragement, support, training, and a lot of work to get that performance. In a world where people can find a job working somewhere else, we are not entitled to their best.

Most managers do not know how to navigate this process.

The employees who will give excellent performance in the current work environment desire a culture where leaders inspire them and do what it takes to guarantee they are successful. This sounds like entitlement on the employee's behalf. However, the reality is when supervisors are leading in a way that guarantees success, the best employees will strive to become their best.

This is where an abundance mindset of leadership comes into play. Leading people without feeling entitled and believing we must earn performance will result in people running through walls for the leader.

We can no longer hire people and sit in our offices and demand that our people give us their best and perform at a high level. We must get out of the office, give clarity, coach, train, provide support, build resources and tools to help, and earn the right for people to bring their best every day. Reverse Performance Leadership is a strong step in the right direction.

CHAPTER 11

FUTURE LEADERS WILL ACT DIFFERENTLY AND WILL BE REQUIRED TO HAVE CERTAIN SKILLS

I am a big fan of Kelly Monahan at Meta. She speaks about future work and has been published on the topic. In 2018 she had already identified the potential shift in management from command and control to development coaching training of employees in her book *How Behavioral Economics Influences Management Decision-Making: A New Paradigm.*

She argued that the behavioral science supports a change where midlevel managers will train and coach people, HR managers will have higher levels of employee development as a job requirement, and people will take responsibility for results and how they get those results.

We are currently seeing a shift from command and control, where we need to address how people do their jobs and micromanage every step, to creating a culture with continuous learners who have critical thinking skills and emotional intelligence attributes, who understand lean thinking, and who are free to get results in the best way possible. We will need to train those people in all that we know and still allow them to fail with new ideas and techniques.

Stephen M. R. Covey recently published *Trust and Inspire: How Truly Great Leaders Unleash Greatness in Others.* If you want to truly understand the mindset, attitude, and character of a great leader in a successful company of the future who moves away from command-and-control management, then read his book. Becoming this type of leader starts with the attitudes taught by Mr. Covey. However, without the clarity of what is expected and a knowledge of how performance will be measured, great leaders and organizations will continue to struggle.

This means we will potentially have to change the people in middle management roles. The skill set for success will be empathy, teaching, coaching, lean systems, and active involvement in the work. When these managers begin ramping up performance of talent, organizations will thrive.

It will take time and tough decisions to shift these roles and, in some cases, people. It will be the tough-minded leaders who will make these changes and thrive.

CHAPTER 12

MANAGEMENT MUST TAKE RESPONSIBILITY

Driving accountability down to the lowest level (which was introduced thirty years ago in management principles) has caused laziness among managers. If accountability is driven down to the lowest level, then management doesn't have to take responsibility for results, doesn't have to respond quickly, and isn't truly driven to get the results required from employees.

Let me explain in more detail. If an operations manager is managing customer service representatives and the CSRs are responsible for getting certificates out on time to a client, what happens if they don't do it? In reality, it takes a long time to move on this because it is not monitored closely or disciplined quickly. It is not the *highest* priority of the manager. If the operations manager were held accountable for the certificates not getting out on time to the client, then the manager would monitor the task closely, work harder to train and encourage the customer service representative to do the right things, and move quickly on firing incompetent people.

Another example. If the sales manager were held accountable for individual performance of producers, how long would he or she tolerate poor behaviors? How long would he or she allow people not to follow the system? How much time would he or she spend helping producers successfully generate business? The bottom line (and I was guilty of this) is that if the accountability is driven down to the employee, then the manager can point the finger and say, "That person is a problem. It isn't my fault." If the president of the company were to look at me and say, "I don't manage the producer, I manage you. And that person's results are what I expect you to manage," it would require me (as the sales manager) to be quicker to train, quicker to discipline, and quicker not to tolerate poor performance.

Let's look at a president. What if the shareholders were to hold the president accountable for the individual performance of his or staff? Would the president then do anything different? I would suggest that he or she would do some things different in terms of speed of decisions, time spent helping employees be successful, and how he or she measured and tracked their daily performance. Just writing that statement convinces me that it is the right thing to do. How long can direct reports look at the president and shrug their shoulders about their people's poor performance? How long can they look at the president and say people are performing just fine? Under most business structures this is tolerated because the manager is not held accountable for the individual performance of their people.

This makes me think of professional sports. Think of an NFL coach, who is responsible for overall results as well as the individual performance of players. If the quarterback is doing a terrible job (even if the team is still winning), the fans, media, and the owner(s) of the franchise will continually hold the coach accountable for the QB's performance.

Here is a list of things that I believe would come from a structure of managers being held accountable for their subordinates' behaviors and results:

1. Quick decisions to eliminate those who don't belong in the organization.
2. A focus of managers to make sure employees have a great work environment to be successful.
3. An encouraging and motivational culture.
4. Better training due to a need to train quickly and thoroughly.
5. Increased amount of coaching. If the coach is accountable for the player's performance, the coach will "coach" the player more often instead of just letting him or her consistently perform poorly.
6. Managers spending more time in the trenches with the troops.

So, what does it mean to be held accountable for employee performance? I believe it means that whatever is used to measure the employee's performance must be wrapped up into the manager's objectives in order to measure the success or failure of the manager. This can only be done if there are objective measurements for employees.

CHAPTER 13

MAKING BETTER MANAGERS/LEADERS BY CREATING SYSTEMS THAT HELP THEM OVERCOME WEAKNESSES

Let's revisit the unfortunate situation we put our managers in with performance reviews.

They spend hours trying to come up with a performance review for each employee. They struggle to prepare because so much is subjective and lacking in certainty. They struggle to give compliments because they don't have the skills to balance properly, and it is a guess as to what should be communicated.

We don't train managers on handling conflict or having difficult conversations. We don't teach them techniques for giving accurate reviews. Managers frequently deliver reviews late for a broad number of reasons, but primarily because they don't want to do them.

Compensation is typically tied to the review. This element of pay and reward stresses those on both sides of the conversation.

The employee is in a terrible place where he or she believes he or she must prepare a counter presentation to defend the quality of work and explain his or her performance.

In such a scenario, both sides are set up to fail.

The fact that this activity exists proves we are failing to give clarity to our employees.

The model of Reverse Performance Leadership eliminates this problem and creates a natural success model for managers to lead great performance.

The manager will show up to the meeting with the sole purpose of helping the employee perform. It is a servant leader model vs. lording-over experience.

When employees are performing well, they can automatically be praised and recognized for this performance. The system automatically draws the discussion because the employee gives evidence of his or her success.

If an item is below standard, the manager can address it quickly because the system is built to trigger correction when the employee is slightly falling short. This allows quick correction, guidance, and teaching to get the employee back on track when nobody is mad and it is able to be repaired.

If the employee falls critically short, the manager gets to support him or her with empathy instead of being the bad guy for informing the employee of this reality.

Meetings can be monthly and take less than thirty minutes per session. In most cases the sessions can be fifteen to twenty minutes. Only when correction or development is needed will the meetings need to go longer.

Leaders give clarity to people on what they need to accomplish and get out of the way, and then make themselves available to train, support, and give the tools for great performance. It is a fun job!

PART III

FIELD GUIDE TO THE REVERSE PERFORMANCE LEADERSHIP SYSTEM

Field Guide

The remainder of *Leading Performance … because It Can't Be Managed* is the how-to segment. We will give clear instructions on writing SMART objectives, creating objective vs. subjective expectations, scoring, and weighting; suggest techniques for review meetings and compensation; and provide numerous examples of successful objectives from innovative companies.

SMART Objectives

SMART is a common acronym for being objective. I have seen many different words used in the acronym. I have used the ones I connected with when I thought through the desired outcomes of performance leadership.

S = specific: Specific means we answer who does what and by when. If necessary, it can also include how something should be done. But be careful not to remove the flexibility and creativity of the employee.

M = measurable: Measurable means something has the ability to be measured. This can be a frequency of behavior, a score, relativity to a standard, or a measurement we invent for the situation.

A = attainable: To be attainable, the outcome must be reasonably reachable for the person. When supervisors give stretch goals or items that set the bar above what a reasonable person can accomplish, it decreases the motivation more often than it inspires. This is why we establish level 5 opportunities (see score later in the book). High standards that are attainable will keep a person focused on the target.

R = relevant: A relevant objective will have a significant and demonstrable bearing on the topic. I have observed many objectives that simply did not align with the objectives or key results of an organization. These objectives were typically something the organization had simply always done, and a bias existed to keep it in place. Good objectives will test against the relevance to the organization's success.

T= trackable: Trackability means the employee can track his or her success at any point. It is not motivating if the measurement is not seen frequently. An employee should be able to see exactly where he or she is in terms of performance at any time.

CHAPTER 14

HOW TO WRITE OBJECTIVE OUTCOMES VS. SUBJECTIVE OUTCOMES

I have trained my consulting partners to write performance objectives. It doesn't take long before they get it and are teaching me new tricks. However, it isn't easy initially. It requires a different thought process, critical thinking skills, creativity, possibly collaboration, and an understanding of certain principles of measurement.

We must start by understanding what outcomes are required. This is very hard because we don't naturally do this with employees in form, but we do it randomly at different times during the year.

I begin by asking questions of the manager:

1. We are at the end of the year. What results must have happened for you to be happy with this person being in this job?
2. What would get this employee terminated based on performance (not including morality issues)?
3. What would get this employee promoted or a pay increase above the norm?
4. What do you find yourself wishing employees in this position would do?
5. What do you find employees in this position doing that you wish everyone else would do?
6. Are you aware of any performance improvements needed in this department or with this person?

When you get answers to these questions, you will begin to form the outcomes and results expected.

However, it does take a lot of practice, collaboration, and grinding out of ideas to measure everything. I believe we can always get there, but we need to put in the work early to make this easier in the long term.

One suggestion is to use critical thinking skills in creating effective measurements. Ask the following additional questions:

- What if we had to measure it? We must find a way.
- How can we measure it?
- Can we measure indirectly?
- Can we build systems on top of each other that create a combined measurement?

Let's take a CFO as an example. The answers to some of the foregoing questions would be as follows:

1. I would want my financials timely (within five working days after the start of the month).
2. I would want the financials to be accurate—no more than two corrections in any month on average.
3. I would want the CFO to know our key vendors to make certain we have good relationships with them.
4. Maybe I would like to see the CFO reduce expenses by 2 percent during the year. If he or she could get to 5 percent with items I approve, that would exceed my expectations.
5. I would like for the CFO to be collaborative and have a good working relationship with the other executive team members.
6. I would like for the CFO to have a relationship and a plan with our CPA and our attorney for key initiatives we are working on as a firm.
7. I would like to see personal development be purposeful because it is a company value.
8. The CFO must work with employees to manage Reverse Performance Leadership with them.

We have included more specific objectives in the appendix and online at our web site for the book. These examples can show more specifics of how to get good SMART objectives.

CHAPTER 15

SCORING RATIONALE AND WEIGHTING OBJECTIVES

The scoring is a magical part of the process but is one of the hardest things to communicate and understand by the employees.

I believe scoring systems should accomplish numerous items that motivate the proper actions.

First, a scoring system must have built-in recognition. People want to be recognized when they do well. This is true even if it is just for one area of performance. I find many supervisors won't recognize someone for doing something well because the person is not doing well in other areas. It is critical to communicate to employees exactly how they are performing and not sway to one side or the other. So, the system must have an objective scoring system that allows for immediate recognition when someone goes above and beyond expected results.

Second, I believe scoring systems should trigger when someone falls slightly short of expectations. In my years of working with managers, I find most of them can't communicate when performance is falling slightly short because the measurement isn't clear at the standard or slightly-falling-short level. It would be hard to tell someone he or she is falling short when the standard isn't clear. It is especially hard when the lag is very minor.

Wouldn't you want to communicate when performance is falling slightly short so you can get things back on track? Why wait until you are mad? Isn't that when you typically have the conversation? You get mad enough and certain enough the employee is failing that you gain confidence to inform him or her that he or she is performing at an unacceptable level.

I believe slightly short objectives allow for quick correction, training, and encouragement, so the employee can get back on track quickly.

One of my clients told me the scoring system should be called the

"Goldilocks Scoring System." He said fours and fives were hot and potentially too hot, respectively, because it would be almost impossible for someone to live in that space full time. He said the ones and twos were too cold and not a place where anyone could live for long. But the score of three was just right!

I thought it was a fun and entertaining story and probably was right on the mark. So, maybe the scoring should be that three is just right!

Let's dig into the detail on the scoring model.

We use a 1–5 rating system. We have tried many systems and have found that the 1–5 model is the most efficient to develop. And it meets all the objectives listed above.

We will start with the level 3 score. A three is the high expectation for the position. It is not an average, and it represents the high level expected for the position.

We have two scores below a three that each have a specific purpose.

A score of two is considered **slightly below the standard expected**. This is very important because it allows the employee and the supervisor to be able to address a performance shortfall quickly before anyone gets mad. This is a critical point of correction that will allow adjustments, training, coaching, and possibly supervisor intervention to eliminate barriers. When a score of two is defined, the employee can respond quickly and get back on track. I have experienced numerous people who have gotten back on track quickly with the awareness of the defined score that showed they were falling short.

A score of one is defined as **falls critically short of expectations**. This is important because the supervisor and employee must be on the same page as to what behaviors or deliverables would result in discipline, corrective action, or unacceptable outcomes.

On the opposite end are the upper numbers of recognition.

A score of four represents **exceeds expectations**. This is an opportunity to recognize when someone is getting desired results above the standard. Remember the story of taking out the trash? These are the items my father told me he wished I would have done, instead of doing the items I chose to do on my own. The four objective will allow for the supervisor to help guide the employee to the best possible results that will give the best outcome for the company.

A score of five is defined as **far exceeds expectations**. This level of objective can be utilized with two different methods.

The first is a very defined item or outcome that falls well above the level 4 objective. This will allow elite performance to be identified if the company is clear on what that would look like. Someone should not have any employee who can reach a five in every category. The core objectives should be set higher. This is built-in recognition and a great opportunity to frequently show appreciation and reward great performance.

The second method for a level 5 score strategy is to leave it open with some direction, suggesting outcomes that give flexibility or even allow the employees to define them. Examples are available in the appendix. Again, recognition is built in and allows supervisors to give recognition frequently.

Now that the scoring structure is clear, we need to adjust for the value of these objectives. Not all performance objectives are created equal. Some items mean more to the firm than others. We must represent that in our scoring system.

Consider a salesperson with a primary job of selling new revenue to new clients. This job is created because of the strategic and tactical need of growth in terms of new clients. Some people would argue that the salesperson should be measured on that one item and nothing else.

My question would be, do you measure anything else, or would you consider any other issues such as performance, promotion, and potentially dismissal?

The initial answer I would expect is, "No, that's it." However, upon further review (quick NFL reference there), the person I'm asking may add a few items. He or she may add that the salesperson must be an active and positive participant in sales meetings and meet all the sales requirements (training, product understanding, and other team activities). This person may be required to sell a balance of products to make certain the most profitable products are being sold. A corporate citizenship component could be required. Many salespeople could benefit from being held accountable for acting responsibly internally. They may be held to an expectation to retain clients or potentially represent the brand in a specific manner in the community.

Clearly a salesperson could do a lot of things well to offset a slow sales year, and he or she could be terminated quickly if all those other areas were weaknesses and sales were not so good.

The point is that we measure a lot of things with people because we expect a lot. Therefore, we must include those items in our performance objectives. But if the employee doesn't do the main thing he or she is hired to do (take out the trash), then his or her performance will most likely not be good enough.

So, in this case we may put a 40–50 percent weight on the sales number; maybe 10–15 percent on client retention; and small percentages on the remaining items.

The math is relatively simple from there. You make the sum of all objectives 100 percent. Then, you take the score of an objective and multiply it by the percentage assigned to that objective. Then, you add up the results, with each of the objectives being included.

Example

Objective 1 = 20%
Objective 2 = 40%
Objective 3 = 10%
Objective 4 = 5%
Objective 5 = 25%

Now we score them:

Objective 1 = score of 2
Objective 2 = score of 3
Objective 3 = score of 2
Objective 4 = score of 5
Objective 5 = score of 5

Now we assign the value to the score for each objective:

Objective 1 = 20% × 2 = 0.4
Objective 2 = 40% × 3 = 1.2
Objective 3 = 10% × 2 = 0.2
Objective 4 = 5% × 5 = 0.25
Objective 5 = 25% × 5 = 1.25

We now add the ending calculations:

0.4 + 1.2 + 0.2 + 0.25 + 1.25 = 3.3

This employee had excellent performance. He or she performed slightly below expectations in two areas but made up for it with excellent performance in the two areas that had the biggest weight.

One of the tests of performance objectives is to model out scoring like this and ask yourself if you would be pleased with this outcome if the employee were to accomplish these results. If the answer is no, then you would need to change the weighting.

Let's say the above scoring entailed 25 percent for objective 3 and 15 percent for each objective 4 and objective 5. The score would then be a 2.7. In that case, the employee would certainly not be in a position of being terminated, but corrective action would occur.

Weighting is a critical part of making sure an employee understands what impact he or she makes in the areas where he or she performs. It gives leaders the ability to emphasize certain outcomes but also allow for other measurable behaviors and results to recognize the performance impact of the employee.

Know that people will initially be very concerned about being scored at a 3 when a 5 is on the sheet. Remind them your culture has high standards for a 3 and 4s and 5s are for built in recognition. This is critical to the success of the process.

Another pitfall is when someone tells you they spend a lot more time on items that have a lower weight. This is not a measurement of time. The measurement is of the value and impact it has on the firm.

So, weights should give someone the ability to see clearly where high impact can be made in the job.

Play with weighting and feel free to make adjustments during the year to get to the right balance of performance. I have used different measurements for different people in the same positions because I needed to influence specific behavior to get improved results. This is a very acceptable strategy. And always remember that you are working toward enhanced performance for desired results.

Fractional Scoring

I am also a fan of fractional scoring in each segment. If someone meets *all* the level 3 objectives and some of the level 4 objectives, I believe manager discretion, with evidence to support the discretionary fraction, is perfectly acceptable.

An easy one: If a salesperson has a $1 million sales goal and $1.2 million is the no. 4 objective, and the salesperson hits $1.1 million in sales, he or she will receive a score of 3.5.

Another example is a manager who has a no. 3 objective of establishing a plan by a certain date and then showing evidence of meeting the plan monthly. The no. 4 objective is to have approved quarterly updates with modifications to improve performance of the division. If the manager does that in one of quarters and meets all the level 3 objectives, he or she could receive a score of 3.25.

However, I want to be clear that this falls in the realm of the "Take Out the Trash" chapter. If the person doesn't do the level 3 objective and does some of the level 4 items, he or she gets *no credit* for the level 4 items and will fall short of the level 3. It is critical that employees stay disciplined in terms of the no. 3 objectives as being the critical items they must accomplish to be successful.

CHAPTER 16

FREQUENCY OF MEETINGS

To move from a lording leader model where you are telling the employee how he or she has performed to a servant leader who is helping the employee realize successful performance requires more frequent and shorter one-on-one meetings.

The annual reviews that took hours to prepare for, caused much stress, and took up much time for the meetings just to attempt to sell the employee on why you like or dislike his or her performance are over. Now you can meet for ten-to-fifteen-minute check-ins to give feedback and support to the employee's self-management. The employee will communicate to you how he or she is doing with evidence to prove the objective results.

You will have the opportunity to praise the employee if he or she is performing above expectations in terms of the different objectives, and give guidance and support where the employee is falling slightly short. If your employee starts falling critically short, you can put him or her into more intense training or corrective action to get him or her back on track.

You no longer have to be the bad guy! You no longer need to deliver bad news. You get to be the person who your employees believe is there to help them!

My recommendation is to have monthly one-on-one meetings that employees are required to initiate. They need to own their performance to that degree. These meetings should be ten to twenty minutes in length, depending on how long you and the other person need to get through the discussion and the time it takes for you to provide support.

Once every quarter you can spend forty-five minutes to an hour with each individual to go deeper, adjust objectives, give more training, celebrate successes, and show how much you care about them.

In some organizations, that forty-five minutes each quarter with fifteen-minute monthly sessions in between will go on forever. No need for the big annual review. You are managing performance ongoing. Isn't that what a performance review is supposed to do?

At one of my leadership positions, I was able to have ten-minute monthly one-on-one sessions with my direct reports. They knew their numbers and measurements so well, they were able to go over the information in three to four minutes. The remaining six to seven minutes gave me time to thank them for excelling in certain areas and to give some support where they were falling short. If they were really struggling and falling dramatically short, I would schedule additional time for training and coaching.

People loved the short check-ins that were all about them. It gave most of my people the chance to tell me how well they were doing and get recognized. This is something most organizations are missing.

CHAPTER 17

COMPENSATION

The natural next question is, What about compensation discussions? I believe compensation should be addressed on employment anniversary dates instead of all at the same time at the first of the year.

A company can establish a compensation strategy each year and follow that strategy throughout the year to make certain that budgets are being managed effectively.

It would take an entire book to address compensation to the full extent. I will address the core principles of compensation and attempt to make connections to performance objectives.

A solid compensation plan will have the following elements:

The first step is to develop a compensation strategy as a company. This strategy includes core values, structural components, competition, and beliefs of how compensation fits in with the corporate strategy.

After strategy is defined, I would research and identify the appropriate compensation structures that fit the job. The structure can consider such facets as salary, hourly wage, bonuses, and commission, and can include deferred compensation and ownership models.

The third step is to tie performance to the compensation model. Performance objectives can be used in the foregoing models to provide clarity for increase ranges and for bonus opportunities. I would avoid giving more compensation in exchange for higher scores as that will cause potential manipulation of scoring or could cause people to be unhappy with the fact that a score of 3 is an acceptable outcome. This could damage a good performance management program.

I have always used the scoring system for my own compensation program. As I practice it, the relationship of compensation to my performance objectives is simply that raises, shares of additional stock, and bonuses simply become available with a minimum performance average score of 3 across all objectives. I have included the requirement of a level 3 in terms of all objectives to reach maximum bonus or raise potential.

Executive compensation can be tied to individual objectives or the entire group of objectives for a job. I encourage creativity in this area. Tying executive compensation tied to earnings alone and/or the stock price is dangerous. Too many outside factors will influence those outcomes and could cause you to pay more than is justified.

In our modern world, where we need to keep the best employees but those employees are our competitors' biggest targets, we need to build golden handcuff models into our compensation strategies. Nonqualified deferred compensation, stock appreciation rights programs, company ownership, and life insurance ownership strategies all need to be considered as an employee will regard it as too large of a financial hit to leave the company.

Do not be lazy on compensation. Use performance leadership models to help justify compensation, but find good experienced counsel on compensation strategy to build sustainable value for the company.

CHAPTER 18

IMPLEMENTATION STRATEGY

I have implemented Reverse Performance Leadership in hundreds of companies. When we start with those at the top of the organization, we have greater success. It is valuable to have the executive team experience the process first. This allows the executives to be more effective when they deliver the system to the employees.

The empathy that comes with understanding how it feels to know the expectations, give feedback to your supervisor, and track your own performance allows for better understanding when explaining to direct reports.

I have maintained my own performance objectives for the past fifteen years. I have business partners and boards of directors whom I have reported to over those years. I write my own objectives and share them with those to whom I am accountable in my job. I review the monthlies, send quarterly updates to those to whom I am accountable, and have discussions with them about my performance. It gives me great energy to see how much more focused I am in performing toward my key objectives with this focus.

When I meet with my team monthly, I am able to have great empathy for them because I am doing the same thing as they are.

Start your process with yourself and run for three months. The next step is to give objectives to your direct reports. Run the feedback for three months with them as well. Continue to go layer by layer in the organization until all employees are on the system.

It is also valuable to teach the employees why you are implementing this program. Start with educating them on the realities mentioned in *Leading Performance … because It Can't Be Managed*. Help them see how bad life is when things are subjective and their managers don't systematically help them perform to their potential.

CHAPTER 19

DEVELOPMENTAL PLANS

Every employee should have a developmental plan, and it should be a performance objective for each employee to purposefully execute that plan. When every employee in a company is improving, the company is improving.

We identified in the opening chapters of *Leading Performance ... because It Can't Be Managed* how employees are looking for opportunities to improve and develop at work. They need the direction, time, and guidance to make those improvements. Building the objective for development as a performance expectation will increase the chance they will take advantage of the development you offer.

Developmental plans can include reading, classes, mentoring, coaching, or program participation. Let the employee help with the discovery of the best avenues for development and the outcomes he or she desires. You make certain the development will benefit the organization.

We also encourage the use of micro learning strategies. Employees typically do not have the time to go to full-day classes. Find avenues where people are able to spend fifteen to thirty minutes in micro learning experiences. The retention of material and the impact will be greater than with longer training and learning environments.

If every employee of an organization is improving a skill, emotional intelligence, mindfulness, or possibly any improvement as a human, the organization improves as a whole. The combination of people wanting to develop and the advantage it can bring to a company certainly should make a formal development program a priority.

Tie it into the performance leadership system so it will become a cultural habit!

CHAPTER 20

HIRING FOR PERFORMANCE-BASED SYSTEMS

If we are going to have elite organizations with elite people who can manage flexibility and manage themselves, then these employees must be performance-based individuals.

Performance-based individuals are not found by way of attendance records, participation trophies, time in an industry, or job history. Performance-based individuals have always won all or most of their lives! These people have found a way to win in sports, in theater, against adversity, in terms of job expectations, and in all areas of life.

I remember my second interview at Ryder. The regional sales manager interviewed me in the Los Angeles airport. He began by telling me it wasn't going to be a traditional interview.

His first question was how old I was when I had my first job. I told him I was twelve and started mowing lawns in the neighborhood. Then at thirteen I started babysitting. He asked me how many times I had been fired for not performing in my job. I told him not once until I went into the NFL, and then I was fired three times in three years. He said that was a different level of getting fired!

His second series of questions seemed to be about my memory. He asked what I remembered about being a young kid in elementary school. I told him about the playground and being the smallest but toughest kid playing all sports. I shared about the positive experiences I had in terms of my relationships with teachers.

He moved the discussion to middle school, and I told him about being in the band, receiving rewards, playing sports, and again about developing great relationships with students and teachers.

My time in college went in a similar direction as I told him about overcoming a down period of not studying and taking college seriously but still making it to graduation. I mentioned playing sports, receiving rewards in my business classes, being president of the Fellowship of Christian Athletes, and other accomplishments that were all pretty cool but mostly about hard work and overcoming size, speed, and lack of natural brainpower!

At the end he asked me if I understood what he had just done with me. I suggested he had just determined if I had a good work ethic, if I had a good memory, and if I had performed well.

He said I was close. He explained that he had not failed in his hiring in the past because of this process. He was looking for the following:

1. Early work start. An early start working usually means a great work ethic. That I had started working at age twelve was pretty good. He said he was looking for either a job or seriously committed sports or academic work that looked like a job before age sixteen.
2. Success. Successful people tend to continue to be successful. That can mean successfully staying off drugs in a neighborhood where all the other kids were on drugs or being the captain of the football team. Success was defined as getting one's best results and not failing.
3. Positives vs. negatives. People who remember positive things tend to be positive people. People who dwell on the negative tend to be negative.
4. Finally, how much gratitude an interviewee had about his or her past. Fortunately, I had mentioned my parents, teachers, and teammates, and great neighbors who let a twelve-year-old mow their lawn.

In the end he told me he had no question I was going to be successful, and he offered me the job.

I believe this regional manager was years ahead of his time. I believe great organizations will attract and retain people who are positive, successful people with a great work ethic who have gratitude for those who helped them get to where they are.

A person who has the flexibility and freedom to manage his or her work will be very successful with these four attributes.

I recommend that you get creative in this journey. Success comes in many forms beyond sports, theater, and privileged opportunity. I have met many people who come from backgrounds much different from mine who exceeded me in all four categories. Diversity is valuable to any firm. Seek people of different backgrounds, belief systems, and educational experiences. These differences will create a strong, smart, and innovative culture.

So, don't look for success that looks like yours. Look for people who are results-focused and experienced. People who are task- and activity-focused will talk about how hard they are working (or worked) and how busy they are. Results people speak of outcomes!

The quality of people you employ will make a big impact on how this system will work for both you and them.

CHAPTER 21

PERFORMANCE LEADERSHIP FINAL THOUGHTS

Leading performance in the modern employment environment requires a major shift in how we lead and operate our businesses. If we desire to get the best talent, we will need to first become the leaders whom people want to follow. This includes giving clarity of expectations, providing time to help our people become their best, and creating magnetic organizations.

To be effective as leaders, we must be creative in thinking through performance results, create systems to tie the performance of connected groups and individuals, and be present to give frequent feedback.

We will also need systems and structure to ensure our leadership is successful. We must build systems for guaranteeing our success, documenting expected results, building review frequency expectations, creating developmental plan models, enabling career pathing, creating compensation strategies, and implementing hiring strategies.

The opportunities for being a leader by title and riding the wave of success will be limited and short-lived. Leadership is a job that will require being purposeful and spending time with people, versus spending time in an office analyzing data and building reports for command-and-control management.

The journey toward the flow of goals, OKRs, performance results, and job descriptions will take time and practice. We are building communities to share ideas and best practices. We encourage you to join in the conversation and to lead performance … because you can't manage it!

Find us on LinkedIn at Linkedin.com/company/intellectual-innovations.

For more tools, ongoing intellectual property, and more, consider joining our ii community at https://intellectual-innovations.com

You can also follow me or Drew on LinkedIn, Instagram, or Twitter (as long as the world keeps them in play).

CHAPTER 22

SUCCESS STORIES OF PERFORMANCE IMPROVED WITH UNIQUE OBJECTIVES

The Flower Shop

A flower shop had nine locations with large differences between profit and sales from one shop to the next. As we went through the process of understanding the profit models, the roles of managers and staff, and the goals of the company, along with determining the performance objectives, the CEO told me he had a hundred-point inspection sheet that he used when he visited the stores. It included things such as picking dead leaves off plants, checking the pricing of every item on the floor, and ensuring the windows were clean and the lights were working. It would take about fifteen minutes to do the inspection.

He went on to tell me how the stores that scored more than 90 percent on a regular basis performed better than the stores that did not.

This opened my eyes to the reality of a measurement opportunity.

He asked me if we should start measuring the manager on the score and make the manager do it daily.

I determined that this would not work because of conflict of interest. I believed the goal would be for a manager to do the inspection daily and be objective. I felt we had two measurement opportunities for performance objectives that would get us greater performance.

We decided the first measurement would be measuring the frequency with which the branch manager did the inspection. This would guarantee awareness of the focus of the key factors of a successful store. The measurement was to show evidence of a store inspection on a minimum of 250 days per year (vacation, sick days, etc., were removed).

The evidence was a folder with the inspection sheets in it with a check mark on the cover sheet and the score posted.

This is a relatively simple measurement, but the outcome was like magic!

The second measurement was that all employees were measured on the average score. The objective was to score about 90 percent of the average score on the daily inspections for the year.

This objective may seem a bit unfair in that all employees were not there every day and were not in control of every item each day. But the culture changed immediately when they knew they were being measured on this objective. There was team accountability for making sure things were done according to the hundred-point check system. If a light was out, someone would fix it immediately. If a dead leaf was hanging on a plant, it was removed. If the floor was dirty, they cleaned it.

They would keep a running total of the average score posted in the back of the store, where all employees could see the results real time.

The result was a sharp movement of increased sales and profit from the stores that were previously lagging behind. All stores went to industry-leading performance. This didn't require any additional marketing or sales training. There was no additional product development. Simply finding the right measurements for the performance that would get results, and letting the two objectives work together, created an outcome of excellent performance!

The Insurance Agency Process Audit

A similar story to the flower shop was an insurance agency that was struggling with service team members either following processes and procedures or potentially not even knowing if they were following the processes and procedures (thus needing training).

We put together an audit process we labelled "ten-minute audits."

The concept was to develop ten steps for monitoring any procedure. We took all the processes and procedures we believed were not being followed consistently and created single-page audit forms (we eventually digitized the process).

Each manager in the service department was given a similar assignment and similar measurements as the flower shop managers. They were asked to do five ten-minute audits weekly. They were required to do audits on account managers' work products or actively ask them to do work that they audited. Each audit had to be able to be done in ten minutes or less (to spend more time on audit wouldn't have been worth the return on time).

When the managers did an audit, they would score the team members according to percentage of successful audit items accomplished. On any item that was not accomplished accurately or with the right process, the manager would do immediate training with the team member. This allowed for processes and procedures to be audited frequently and accomplished successfully, with real-time training.

Again, the managers were scored only on frequency of audits. They had to accomplish this five times per week. They could do all five in an hour or do one audit per day. It was up to them, according their schedule.

The second measurement was the individuals being audited. The account managers and assistant account managers were measured on the average score throughout the year. The objective was to score 95 percent or better throughout the year to meet the 3 objective. A score of 4 would equal 97 percent, and a score of 5 would equal 100 percent. A score of 2 would be the result of 90–94 percent, and a score of 1 would be an average throughout the year at 89 percent or less.

The service team members were aware that every scoring audit would matter.

The result was a very quick request from all account managers to make certain they understood the audit measurements. They were all given quick training and given the audit sheet that would be used when they were audited.

The results were incredible. The firm started with a constant frustration that processes and procedures were not being met or accomplished frequently throughout the organization. Immediately upon putting this system in place, the audits were averaging more than 95 percent from the start. Everyone took note of the measurement and the training and sharpened their skills and discipline to execute. In the last half of the year, the scores were 100 percent on every audit.

This performance objective and process created a 100 percent adoption and execution of proper processes and procedures.

The Construction Company

This is one of my favorite stories of measurement and of making certain the right things are measured!

A large masonry contractor had grown incredibly quickly. The CEO was a friend, and I was an adviser to him. We were talking one day about his growth and how tired he was of running the company. He asked me what I thought about his potentially hiring a general manager. He felt it was time to bring in a GM who could take over the running of the business, which would allow him to be more strategic and slow down a bit.

I told him I thought it was a great idea, and I actually found him a great GM who could run his company.

The CEO decided to put Reverse Performance Leadership in place, and he and I wrote the objectives. He was extremely committed to safety and to workers staying focused in an injury-free workplace. Hauling around block, brick, and stones can be very hard on the body, and injuries can happen fast.

The CEO had always made safety his highest priority and even required toolbox talks on safety before every job started, along with safety checks and monthly safety meetings. And managers could make any decision they felt necessary to create a safe work environment.

When we were writing performance objectives for this new manager, the CEO was very concerned about the cost of that big new salary. So, he forgot about safety and decided he wanted a strong ROI. This meant we needed to place productivity as one of the highest-weighted items on his list of objectives.

We determined that since the GM was not doing nearly as much as the CEO used to do, he would easily be able to find improved work productivity with the labor. So, more than 50 percent of his performance objectives consisted of a quantifiable measurement of increased profit per labor hour.

The new manager went from job to job and preached productivity—more block installed per hour, per person. He became a real driver of productivity and was pushing record highs in block installed per labor hour.

However, the injuries went up fast. People were not thinking safety. They were working faster, and their fingers were getting smashed, blocks were being dropped on their feet, and back injuries were happening frequently.

When we measured the cost of this change, we found that it increased productivity with more than five hundred thousand dollars increase in profit year over year. However, insurance costs went up because of injury claims. This was the result of the company having a risk retention program that allowed for profit share with low claims. But with the injury frequency, reserves, and payouts, the retention was lost and the rates went up. The combination cost the company more than one million dollars.

We shifted objectives the next year to 25 percent productivity and 35 percent safety measurements (frequency of injury reduction and following a proactive safety plan). Other measurements were profit, sales, Reverse Performance Leadership for staff, and community involvement.

It took three years to completely reverse the workers' compensation results, but the profit numbers started reversing course again the first year after the objectives were changed. Within three years, the company was making more than one and a half million dollars in increased profit with the new manager.

This is a great lesson in being careful about what you measure because you may get what you ask for, but not want.

The Receptionist

A company we engaged back in the early 2000s was very excited about a Reverse Performance Leadership program. However, they couldn't come up with any ideas for how to measure the receptionist.

We did some research on the type of business and the value the receptionist contributed toward the goals of the company. We identified that the company had increased sales when the receptionist captured certain information. We also identified feedback from client surveys on satisfaction with the receptionist, which made an impact.

We came up with ten things a receptionist could do to make a call productive and maximize the potential with a client. These included things like answering the phone in three rings or fewer, getting the client's name, getting his or her company name, and asking whom the client wanted or needed to speak to in the firm. If the client didn't know whom to speak to, then the receptionist would ask specific questions about what the client needed or wanted. If the person whom the client wanted or needed to speak to wasn't available, the receptionist would ask if the client wanted to leave a voice mail, have someone call him or her back, and so forth.

The ten items were documented, and we trained the receptionist. We hired a retired person from our industry to make one call per week to each of the ten locations where we had receptionists. This person would call, record the call, and make certain all ten items were hit. The average score for the receptionist was the score received for the performance objective. The goal was an average of 95 percent complete.

When we started the program, we had average scores in the seventies. By three months, every location was scoring above 90 percent.

We also did a client satisfaction survey where we asked questions about the front desk and our phone management. Those scores were also part of the receptionist objectives.

A third score was related to the projects we gave the receptionists. They had time while on the front desk to do additional work. When someone brought the work, that person and the receptionist would negotiate the time the latter would need to get that project back. The project was signed in and signed back out. If the project met the time commitment, the receptionist received a check. If it was short of the time frame, the receptionist received an *x*. We had a lot of issues with projects not getting done on time and no proactive communication. This completely changed after putting this segment into place.

Once again, measuring results that matter toward the company objectives was successful with some creative methods of measurement.

The Construction Equipment Company

The CEO of a construction equipment company was very upset with his general manager one afternoon. He said, "Six months ago we wrote off twenty-four thousand dollars in parts inventory because it was out of balance. Today, I was told our inventory is off another thirty thousand dollars. Either we are not placing parts on our maintenance and repair work orders or someone is stealing parts."

I knew our people and knew there was no way we had a thief, and I was confident our internal mechanics were putting parts on the repair orders using proper procedures. What I wasn't certain of was that our mechanics who worked out of trucks were managing parts.

So, we decided to put a performance objective on the field mechanics and the parts manager.

The parts manager's objective was to track all parts received by field mechanics as a separate report and reconcile every month with billings and inventory on trucks. Reconciliation had to be 100 percent. The parts manager's bonus was made available or not based on his meeting his performance objectives. This changed his behavior to require all field mechanics to check in with him or a parts sales team member to receive any parts from inventory.

The field mechanics were also given a unique objective: "No more than 1 percent write-off on parts you check out during the year." This meant they not only had to do a better job of recording what they received, but also had to make certain they included the parts received in the billing and locked their trucks to keep others from stealing parts from their trucks.

The immediate result was 100 percent accuracy on parts inventory and zero write-off on parts. Once again, the behaviors were identified, the process was put in place, and the performance was measured.

We were able to put a bonus plan in place to reward our field mechanics for this result. The improvement in inventory controls and billing process when mechanics checked out parts saved us money and we became an industry leader in inventory management.

The Insurance Agency Elite

An insurance agency had a problem with a group of talented but very difficult-to-manage executives.

The position being led was that of account executive. These are executives with the responsibility of managing a group of insurance clients. They are required to have a very high level of insurance knowledge, great client relationship management skills, and the ability to organize the workflows of account managers supporting their client insurance renewals.

This group is confident and typically have very strong personalities. I was hired as a consultant to build the performance management system for this agency. After I had written all the performance objectives and trained the firm on Reverse Performance Management, the firm offered me a job to lead the consulting practice and lead sales for the organization. I accepted the job.

The first day on the job, we had a management meeting to talk about the account executives. The meeting started with the COO suggesting she didn't want to manage the AEs because they were tough to manage. She said they were demanding, unreasonable, often arrogant about their knowledge and perceived unique experiences, and simply hard to manage. She suggested they acted more like producers (salespeople) and said that as the new VP of sales/consulting, I should take them on my team.

Thinking it was a great opportunity to prove that the Reverse

Performance Leadership model would be successful at managing high performers, I accepted the challenge.

I met with the nine AEs and shared the objectives with them. They talked through every objective (see the example in the appendix) and agreed those objectives were fair and measured the right results. I gave instructions on the monthly one-on-one meeting structure and said that they were responsible for doing the measuring and showing me evidence of how they were doing.

The next month we set meetings for the entire group. These meetings were twenty minutes back-to-back for the first month.

The meetings began with me asking each person to tell me what was on the list of objectives and how they were performing. Not one person could remember anything on the list or had anything prepared.

I pulled out the objectives and reminded them of the objectives. It was as if they hadn't believed this was really going to happen. It also showed the reality of past poor performance management systems. When people can't even remember what is being measured, how in the world can they be successful in performance?

The second month was better, but still the AEs did not meet the mark. All AEs had some information and could remember the items, but they were not prepared with evidence of their performance. They were looking to me to tell them how they were doing. I reminded them again of their responsibility to manage their own performance and provide evidence, that is, quantifiable results.

The third month was magic. They each came in prepared with evidence. They were on track and were performing excellently. The results were more focused. Every one of them had a great attitude because the recognition was built in and they could quantify the results they were getting that helped the organization.

This continued through the end of the year. This group became clear top performers, great team members, and highly engaged employees.

In December the board met to talk about the year, staffing, performance, etc. The tone had completely changed. The COO started the staffing discussion by mentioning her desire to take over the AEs again. She said it was a mistake to have moved them to me because they really needed to be in the same line of communication with the rest of the service staff. She felt that they had become such leaders that they would positively impact the other service roles.

I conceded and allowed the change. All around, this was another success story for Reverse Performance Leadership!

The Insurance Agency Not-So-Bad Guy

An insurance agency had a very high-performing producer-adviser (salesperson). He (Mike) had a very large client base (book of business) of more than one and a half million dollars in annual revenue for the firm. His client count was just over seventy-five clients.

Mike was the primary contact person for these clients, and the clients loved him. He had a great personality and was incredibly attentive and engaging with his clients.

The problem came when Mike worked with his internal team and the rest of the insurance agency personnel. Mike was a tyrant! He was demanding and intolerant, had unrealistic expectations, and caused people more work because of his disorganization and randomly changing expectations. He was rude and abusive when working with anyone internally.

The agency had a problem. They were having frequent meetings about Mike. Staff were quitting, which required the firm to constantly be hiring for his team. Employees would come to management in tears because of his having been unreasonable and rude to them. He was creating a seriously hostile work environment.

Mike had been spoken to and put on notice numerous times. But the firm continued to make excuses for him and simply dealt with the turnover and employee frustration.

When I met Mike, I asked him if he knew the damage he was causing. Of course, he blamed the firm for not providing him the best talent. I was able to show him that he may have been causing some of the problems with his behaviors. He moderately accepted my assertions and was willing to work on making some adjustments. But I knew we needed more than an "I'll try."

I reasoned with him to help him understand that the company could train and develop talent if the talent were willing to stick around long enough to get that training. But his abusive behavior in how he dealt with these issues was causing the turnover. He reluctantly accepted that he had some culpability for this issue.

I also challenged him by saying that he never spoke to a client the way he was speaking to internal people. I asked him to start treating internal people like he treated his clients. He agreed.

With all that was analyzed and all that he agreed to do, I still knew we needed performance management measurements to truly change Mike's behavior and performance. I came up with a strategy of measuring the frequency of meetings caused by Mike or addressing the issue of Mike. The objective was, "You are allowed a total of three meetings about you during the twelve months of the year." I knew we were asking a lot of Mike to go from about twenty-plus meetings a year to zero, so we made three the number for transition.

He objected initially because he felt that many of the meetings were called because people didn't like hard work or didn't want to live up to his standards. I challenged him by saying that he needed to deal with those situations with grace and training and not be intolerant and abusive.

I also reminded him that he adjusted his behavior when clients were unhappy, unreasonable, or demanding, and at times when they were not on the same page as he was. Being a smart guy, he accepted that argument as well.

We also told him that the consequences of not meeting this objective would be progressive outcomes. If he hit four meetings, he would be required to forgo 15 percent of his commission. I told him that he would be the one to pay for the cost of management time. If he hit more than six meetings, his commission would be reduced by the 15 percent and he would be required to start doing some of the service work himself. He would also not receive any replacement team members when someone was lost on account of his behaviors.

He didn't like it, but I asked him if he really expected to continue to have the company call meetings about him. He understood my position and agreed.

We went two months with no meetings. It was great, and his team actually made proactive comments to managers about his improved responses to issues and problems. Just after the beginning of the third month, he blew up at a service person.

"That's one meeting," I told Mike. "You have two more to go in ten months. I would be careful if I were you!"

He was careful. He made it to the six-month mark, then he made another internal mess with his team. Interestingly enough, it was because he messed up a commitment for a client and he became intolerant of his team in how they were working to fix the problem.

"That's two, Mike!" I informed him. "You'd better get focused because you have a lot of time left."

November came around and he had another outburst that made one of his team members feel disrespected. There was a big difference in this situation though. It was much calmer, and the response from the account manager was quite a bit less emotional than in the past. I believe Mike's softening had allowed the team members to engage with each other with more trust. He was building relationships and learning the value of managing his emotions, training vs. complaining, and the team had become less defensive (though it wasn't their responsibility to do so).

Mike made it to the end of the year. His team gave very positive reviews of him as a teammate at the end of the year, and he learned new behavior.

Once again, performance was led through a process of measuring the right things.

Mid-level Manager

I was working with a financial advising company, and they were frustrated with the operations manager. They didn't feel that the operations manager was making strategic progress in developing the operations structure, the client experience, and the productivity of the organization.

The manager worked very hard but tended to be reactive and random in what she developed.

The CEO asked me to help her be more strategic and execute with more productivity.

After interviewing her, I realized she was simply missing clarity on what strategy and execution looked like to the CEO.

I developed a performance objective for her that gave her great clarity. The expectation was to develop an approved strategic plan for operations that included productivity improvements, technology enhancements, new training, improved client experience, and expense reduction from operations by December 15 of the upcoming year. She was also to have monthly targets and objective items in the project implementation and show evidence every month of the measurable progress on each item.

Level 4 was to enhance the plan quarterly based on results. Level 5 was subjective based on hitting level 5 in other objectives tied to these activities. Level 2 was to finish the plan late or miss more than three months of communicating progress. Level 1 was to finish the plan more than ninety days late and/or miss more than five months of communicating results/progress.

The operations manager received the objective and asked me for help and guidance in putting the plan together. She developed the plan and used Monday.com to create project plans for every one of the key areas. This allowed for collaborative visual capabilities for her and the CEO to see the progress.

She developed a great plan and executed 100 percent of the objective. The CEO was thrilled with her performance, and it made a measurable impact on the business.

Performance Management Execution

One of the most effective objectives in this system is the ability to put the measurable responsibility for coordinating and executing monthly updates and personal development on the employee.

An early client put a Reverse Performance Leadership system in place and called me a few months after kickoff. She said, "We are failing in execution. Our managers are not setting times to meet with their teams to do monthly feedback. We keep reminding them, but they just can't seem to make happen."

This is one of the common pitfalls of all organizations. Asking a manager to set up meetings with numerous people tends to overwhelm the manager. It is hard for one person to manage.

Some managers (like me) set aside a couple of hours (up to four in some cases of my career) and schedule people to come in every ten to fifteen minutes (depending on the number of people). But this doesn't work for everyone. It can also be a challenge for employees to be available at those times.

In this case, I suggested the company add a performance objective to every employee. The objective for level 3 was "You are responsible to set and have a meeting with your supervisor monthly to review your performance." The objective weight was only 5 percent, but that would be a great bonus performance area if the employee would simply get it done.

Level 2 was to miss more than three months of the year. Level 1 was miss more than five months during the year. Level 4 was to meet the level 3 score and enhance the meeting with strong evidence and research supporting the performance that increased the efficiency of the meeting. Level 5 performance was to meet the level 3 and level 4 objectives and to show evidence of high energy around performance improvements, making the meeting collaborative, and giving feedback to the supervisor on ways to help support the employee's performance.

The company immediately added this objective and immediately had strong compliance in execution of performance review meetings monthly.

I have found that people have a desire to do the right things and want to perform at the highest level possible. When we give clear expectations and highlight what is important, they will find a way to execute.

The Client Experience Measurement

My company has followed companies like Ritz-Carlton and Disney in terms of our model for managing the client experience. We have created icons that represent the training we have provided in specific areas to ensure our clients feel the way we want them to feel when they engage with us.

The icons are Goldilocks (just right), Sherpa (guides to desired results), Four Seasons Concierge (don't point to outcomes; walk the client there), Einstein (make the client feel we have done our homework and are smart), and Remarkable (the client tells others about the experience because it was unique and amazing).

We have a unique way of measuring the client experience other than surveys. I believe it has made a major impact on our organization and our clients. The objective is to give three examples every month of specific client experiences that represent the icons of our client experience.

I know this sounds crazy. How do we know if those experiences were accurate, effective, or potentially made up?

My response is that I don't care. First, I hire people I can trust. If they lie, I will eventually find out and they will no longer be on the team. But that has never happened. Second, I am not concerned if the accuracy or the effectiveness is exact. What I want is for every team member to be able to recite the icons off the tops of their heads. I want those icons to be second nature to them. Language drives culture! Frequency of items being addressed will eventually make them a reality.

A person could go to any of my team members and find they are able to recite the icons and express with passion how they implement them in their daily activity.

We are a consulting company. I frequently hear that our people represent the icons perfectly. We also have the highest rate of client retention of any consulting firm I have ever known. We have a month-to-month contract with our clients, and our average client has been with us for more than twelve years.

I am confident our client experience is consistent because of this objective for all team members.

The Almost-Termination

I had an employee in one of my branches at the heavy construction equipment dealership who was a great young man. However, he was simply not cut out for the work he was doing. He had been part of the company long before I became his manager and had been told he was doing just fine for a few years. But his performance didn't support his compensation. The lazy manager before me had just let the poor performance exist because it was easy to do so.

The employee was unhappy because his performance was very far below that of all the other people in his role. He knew something wasn't good, and he was confused about the difference between him and the people in his role at other branches. When I first took over as his leader, he made comments about how his manager treated him different. He suggested it was because he was Native American, and the manager was white.

I was obviously concerned about this, first because I felt he needed to be treated fairly and I did not want any racist behaviors or perceptions to be part of a company with which I was involved. Second, it was my responsibility to protect the company, make sure we were doing the right things, and ensure we could defend our actions in court if need be.

I was able to give this employee clear objectives and explained the need for him to meet those objectives and results in order to justify what the company was paying him. I spent time with him to make certain he was given a proper and fair chance to be successful.

We did our best to provide him the training and tools to be successful, and his performance did slightly improve. But, as I had already identified, he simply didn't have the personal skills to be successful in this job.

He came to me in the third month of Reverse Performance Leadership and said he was very concerned about his ability to accomplish the objectives. I asked him if he felt they were fair, and he responded positively, saying that they were absolutely reasonable.

He told me about the poor performance, and we coached him with an eye toward more improvements.

The next month he came to me and said, "I am not able to meet these objectives. I checked to make certain they were consistent with those of other people in my job. I saw that my expectations were below those of my peers in many areas. I know these are fair, but I just can't get these results. What can we do?"

I compassionately told him we had a few options. The first option was that we help him find another job in the company. He didn't think he wanted to do anything else though. The second option was to help him find another job elsewhere. I was able to negotiate with him a resignation with fair compensation, and I helped him with identifying a new place to work.

I believe we were able to get him out of the position within a reasonable time frame, protect the company, treat him with respect and honor, and find him quality employment. We were able to change the perception of racism and discrimination by being consistent and showing compassion toward him. Reverse Performance Leadership created a win for him and for the company.

APPENDIX

CAN WE WEAVE REVERSE PERFORMANCE LEADERSHIP INTO OUR LIVES (FAMILY)?

When I learned the importance of giving clear expectations, I found it works in all relationships.

Spouses become angry because, having hoped the other spouse would do something "because they loved them," are disappointed when it doesn't happen.

Parents become upset when children don't guess correctly at the parents' expectations.

After learning the principles of Reverse Performance Leadership, I consider it more accurate to say, "You don't love me if you hold me accountable to outcomes which you require me to guess at."

Yes, even the most basic things you believe are common sense should be communicated. If you don't want clothes put on the floor, then tell the person that is the expectation. If you want help doing chores around the house, you should ask.

It is a much different violation of relationship respect when someone doesn't do what you ask them to do versus their not doing what you hoped they would do.

My wife and daughters are not perfect at this, but we have a rule that states, "If you do not give clarity in terms of what you expect, then you can't hold someone else accountable for doing it. But when you give clear expectations, and especially if those expectations are agreed upon, a consequence can follow without question."

We have a fraction of the disagreements and arguments that most families have. We just know what is expected and we meet those expectations. We show our love by communicating what we will hold each other accountable to do, instead of holding people accountable for what we hope they figure to be our expectations.

This reality will hold true in associations, in organizations, with boards of directors, with friends, and anywhere a relationship exists. We have expectations of each other, and we should be clear as to those expectations if we are truly going to hold someone accountable for meeting them.

Shift your thinking toward showing your love by being clear about what is expected, instead of thinking someone will show you his or her love by thinking how you think and guessing what you expect. You will find more love that way!

Performance Objective Examples

Go to Theiionline.com to download multiple examples of performance objectives built on the Reverse Performance Leadership™ system.

ABOUT THE AUTHORS

A microeconomist entrepreneur helping business leaders accomplish what they didn't know to be possible, Larry G. Linne has spent thirty-five years working *on* the world of business so his clients can be great at working *in* the business. This work is based on successfully working *in* business as well. He is not just an idea consultant; he is a proven results consultant.

Larry is considered a thought leader in areas of executive development, leadership, personal branding, performance management, and business growth strategies. His microeconomics and behavioral science skills, combined with endless hours of research and connecting dots, allow him to guide people to very safe innovative futures.

His unique abilities are distributed through his work at InCite Performance Group and Intellectual Innovations. These companies consistently create intellectual property that help businesses and individuals reach results they didn't know were possible.

Specialties: microeconomics, behavioral science in sales and economics, performance management, business perpetuation planning and execution, business continuation, executive-level individual productivity, personal branding, corporate branding, first- and second-in-command leadership, executive development, business planning, visioning, sales, marketing, CEO performance and coaching, financial control and operations modeling, public speaking, and presentation skills development.

Drew Yancey, PhD, is president at InCite Performance Group, a leading risk-management advisory firm that helps leaders work on their business so they thrive in it. He leverages extensive strategy consulting and executive leadership experience across multiple industries to guide clients to solving challenging problems at the nexus of risk, strategy, and innovation.

His career started in the food industry as the director of strategy for a Top 50 food service distributor, helping to lead the company through its acquisition by a Top 5 distributor. He then became CEO and led the turnaround of a produce merchandising and distribution company. After that, he was a consultant at Clareo, helping Fortune 500 clients create new growth paths.

Drew has been actively involved in several industry and professional associations throughout his career as a member, leader, and adviser. He earned a Master of Divinity from Denver Seminary, an MBA from Texas A&M University, and a PhD from the University of Birmingham (UK). Drew is an avid traveler (having visited nearly forty countries) and a proud seventh-generation Coloradoan, where he lives with his amazing wife and three kids.

Printed in the United States
by Baker & Taylor Publisher Services